George LeRoy Bennett

Troubled
Footsteps

DORRANCE PUBLISHING CO., INC.
PITTSBURGH, PENNSYLVANIA 15222

ISBN: 978-0-8059-7675-5
Library of Congress Control Number: 2007943392

Printed in the United States of America

First Printing

For more information or to order additional books, please contact:
Dorrance Publishing Co., Inc.
701 Smithfield Street
Third Floor
Pittsburgh, Pennsylvania 15222
U.S.A.
1-800-788-7654
www.dorrancebookstore.com

I dedicate this book to my grandchildren.

This is a beautiful summer day, and here I am again in my old Ford truck riding to visit my mother in a small southern town in Ohio where I was born and raised. My thoughts as I'm driving are always the same as I'm getting closer to my old home: How did my siblings and I ever survive? My childhood was so bad; no child should have to be subjected to the treatment we all received. As I pull into town, the buildings haven't changed much, other than some of the bars have closed over the years, and they have more flowers and trees throughout the street to make it look a little prettier. But the same families and people whom I knew as a child still live there. There is a new restaurant on the main drag, so to speak, owned by my cousin; I'm happy for him that he is able to have that. I wonder if his family remembers the things that prey on my mind and have stayed with me for my whole life.

As my mind wanders, I think back to days that a child or an adult should not have to remember.

My most pleasant memories are staying with my grandfather in the old farmhouse in the country on the outside of Greenfield. I, of course, am not an only child. At this time, I had an older brother and sister, but not all of us stayed with Grandpa, just me. I loved my grandpa, and I was his favorite grandchild. I don't know whether it was because I almost died when I was an infant from meningitis or because we just understood each other. We had an old dog called Rocka Bone, and he followed me everywhere I went. He was my best friend, other than grandpa; he followed me everywhere I went, and several times they found me asleep in the doghouse with Rocka Bone. He used to sleep with Grandpa and me. Grandpa didn't want him to do so, but I would cry so Grandpa would let the old dog sleep with us.

As time passed there would be three more siblings born, a brother and two sisters who are part of the Bennett clan. At this time, the family was Kenneth and Wanda Bennett with children David, Sue, me (George), Kenneth Daniel, Bonnie, and Georgie. My dad and mom bought a house on Paint Street, but I still spent a lot of time with my grandfather. The house had an apartment upstairs where my Aunt Edna and Uncle Buster lived. I'm not sure, but I think they lived there for free. My dad was a good provider; we never went hungry or needed clothes, but I still liked being with my grandpa. He would sit on the porch with his shotgun and tell me he was waiting for the Indians. I didn't know till I was older he was talking about my dad and uncles. My mother also had a brother, Pete. They all ran around together getting drunk, fighting in the bars, and causing a ruckus.

Christmas was a fun time at Grandma and Grandpa's. They always had a large Christmas tree, and the wood stove/coal stove made the house warm and cozy. One Christmas, my mom and dad thought it would be funny to wrap me up and give me as a gift to Grandpa for Christmas, but it backfired because Grandpa wouldn't give me back. So I stayed with them until Grandpa passed away. There were always kids there on the farm: lots of cousins, my mom and her sisters, and their husbands. The other kids and I would get into all kinds of trouble, and everyone got a whipping but me cause I was so small.

Some of the things the kids and I did were really bad, and we probably could have gotten hurt. I remember my older brother and my cousin Paul took pitchforks and killed a lot of the neighbor's pigs because they were mad at him. Boy, did Grandpa give them a whipping for that fiasco. Another time my cousin stole some matches and cigarettes; she was older than me. We got in Grandpa's car, and she lit the match and threw it. I guess she thought it would go out the window, but it went to the back seat and burnt the car to the ground. We didn't get hurt. My cousin Jo got a whipping, but Grandpa only yelled at me because I was the youngest. He knew I would not do that again, but Jo was older and should have known better.

I don't remember when it was, but Grandma and Grandpa had to move out of the old house and to town with my mom, dad, sisters, and brothers; Grandpa was sick and couldn't keep up with the wood stove and such. I'm not sure, but I think I was about five years old. And of course, nothing changed; I always slept with Grandpa, like I did at the farmhouse. One morning when I woke up first, like I always did, I tried to wake Grandpa, but he had died in his sleep next to me.

I knew that something was wrong by the way all the grown-ups where acting, crying, and screaming. Mom and Dad took me upstairs so I couldn't see what was going on, but I knew something had happened. I can't remember much about the funeral; I don't think they let me go. So then I was at home with Mom. Dad, Grandma, and my brothers and sisters.

We were living in Greenfield, and for the first time I can remember, I had friends other than my brothers, sisters, and cousins to play with. My best friend was Henry Penwell, and we played together every day, along with Gary Grate, whose father was a barber in town. While we were small and playing, I had a bad accident. I was playing at the Grate's house, and my sister Sue told me to run across the street. When I did, I was hit by a car. I was in a body cast from my waist down for about a year. I remember going to therapy for a long time, learning how to walk again, and I was in the hospital on and off for a year. My family told me the car had hit me twice.

My oldest brother used to give my mom and dad a real bad time. He is five years older than me, and he would run away with his friend Joe Penwell. They would steal. Other than that, we had a good life at this time of our lives.

At this time, there was David, Sue, and me. I don't know what happened or why, but my dad went to prison in London, Ohio for eighteen months. When he came home, my brother Daniel was born. My dad knew he wasn't his son, even though he was named Kenneth Daniel. My brother didn't find out that my father was not his till he was forty years old or so. That is what I call a well-kept secret between my mother, her sisters, her brother, and of course my father. Some of my aunts took that secret to the grave with them; they never told anyone. And my father never treated Daniel any differently than the rest of us kids, even though he knew he was not his true son. My hat goes off to him for that. My mother finally did tell Daniel who his real father was. He was able to meet him, and there was a resemblance that showed they were related. His real father has passed away since then, and so did mine. Mom decided to tell Daniel; she was afraid she may die, and he would never know who his father was.

We all continued to live on Paint Street, and Mom had two more children with my father. She had Bonnie and Georgie, making six living children. I say that because Mom had lost several children in between. It was never quite clear what happened between them. Some of it was caused by family, and both wanted to go out and party. My dad fooled around, and so did my mom. Before long they divorced.

This is when all the bad things began to happen to me, my brothers, and my sisters.

After the divorce, Mom and us kids moved to Washington Courthouse, Ohio, and Grandma went and stayed with my Uncle Pete. One day my Uncle Pete brought a friend of his, Nolan Simpson, to our house; Uncle Pete brought him from Kentucky from an orphanage. I can remember to this day him walking down the street and walking into our house. That was a bad day, but we had no idea how bad it was going to be.

It wasn't long after that day he walked in that he moved in, and it didn't take him long to show his authority over us kids. In fact, he got outright mean.

We were having a hard time. Mom was on welfare, we were without electricity off and on, and food was very scarce. We used to eat beans of some kind seven days a week, most of the time without seasoning, along with water biscuits. My grandmother was with us off and on; sometimes she was with Uncle Pete. We took baths out back in a washtub. And at times, we would run back and forth to Aunt Mamie's to eat beans and fried potatoes; sometimes we would even have hot dogs. My cousins Michael and Rowdy could reach into the pot of boiling water, grab a hot dog, and never burn themselves. Then they would run so Aunt Mamie couldn't catch them. I tried to grab one out of the pot, but I never could do it. The water was just too hot. We spent a lot of time with the Greens then. My brother David and my cousin Terry got into a fight. David cut Terry's throat, and my mom and Aunt Mamie didn't speak for thirty years. David and Terry never stayed mad at one another. Before Mamie passed away, we all got along very well, and Wanda, my mother, and Mamie forgave each other.

One Sunday my mother and Nolan were fighting, and my brother David tried to shoot Nolan with a high-powered rifle. My mother stopped him. This gun would shoot sometimes, and other times it would not. It wouldn't shoot this day. My mother grabbed it. David then threw kerosene all over the stairwell because Nolan ran up the steps. Then he lit it. I remember them struggling to put the fire out, and he did get it out.

Sometimes when we would go to my Aunt Mamie's, my Uncle Dean would be there. He would make pigs in a blanket, and that was like eating a T-bone steak. We never had much food, and there were no sweets. We would go to school at Christmastime and get a bag of candy. It was a little school called Cherry Hill. One of the most embarrassing times at school was when they pulled me out of school in front of all the kids to take me to get a pair of shoes. My feet were cold, for in the winter we didn't have any money to buy them. So the school would buy them. They would take us back to class in front of all the kids, and they all knew what they did. They could see the shoes. I asked the people who took us why they did that in front of the other kids, and I asked why they couldn't do that in the evening, after school, or on a Saturday. Every day going home I would fight because our clothes were worn out and trashy. We had to go to the creek out behind the house to wash and get drinking water.

On Christmas Santa came to school and gave us all a present. I got little guns, and I took them home. My stepdad Nolan stomped them in the floor; he broke them and threw them away. I always wondered why he did that. They say my stepdad was treated badly in the children's home, so maybe that's why he always treated us badly. I don't know.

At nighttime it would get dark, and we didn't have any electricity most of the time, nor did we have kerosene for the lanterns. So we sat on the porch and told ghost stories. That always seemed like a really good time. Then we would all go to bed, mainly because we had no TV or radio. I thought everyone lived like that.

When we would do something wrong, we would get a whipping with a switch till our legs would bleed. We would have stripes from our backs to our toes. We would be so bloody that they wouldn't let us take gym; they would send us with a note. To think about it now, I guess they didn't want the school to see some of the whippings and how bad they were.

I remember when things didn't go right, we would have to stand in the corner for hours at a time. Sometimes Nolan put an apple on our heads; if it fell, we got a whipping, and then he would put the apple back on our heads. We would have to stand there; even if we had to go to the bathroom so badly, he would not let us go. I had whippings with garden hoses, had wrenches and coffee cups thrown at me, was threatened with razors, and was beaten with switches; my brothers and sisters ensured these things too. He never whipped his own children. They would lie about us, and we would get the whippings.

We finally moved out on State Route 41 toward Greenfield. It was a fairly nice farmhouse. Nolan was supposed to work for free rent, half a cow, and a hog every year. But he never did work; he moved in and didn't do a thing. Our renter was Lauren Johnson; he was a very nice man. We stayed there for five years, and I don't think we ever paid that man a dime for the rent. Again my grandmother Edith stayed with us. We didn't get beaten that much cause Grandma would scream and yell at Nolan to leave us alone.

During the winter we got rabbit and pheasant, which was good. We would have a Thanksgiving dinner and cook what we caught. The winters seemed very, very cold, and our only heat was a wood stove. Still most of the time, we went without electricity. We got our water from an outside well, and the bathroom was half the length of a football field. Nolan would not get out of bed; his bed was by the stove. We were upstairs, so there was not much heat for us. There were no registers in those days, so people cut holes in the floor upstairs so the heat would rise. But not Nolan; he was so lazy. He wouldn't get out of bed till my mother built the fire. To this day, I do not understand why she loved him the way she did. Daniel, my two sisters, and I would be whipped every day. I don't think a day passed when we weren't knocked down.

Nolan and my mother would take the Simpson kids to town to some friends, the Carters. Squirt and her family would eat while we sat at home hungry without food. We would get up in the morning and try to get a piece of bread to sop up the grease in the skillet that was sitting on the stove from the night before when they ate. We got commodities, but I don't know what would happen to them. All I remember that we ate was potted meat and powdered eggs, which wouldn't last long.

In the morning before school, my little brother Daniel and I had to feed the pigs, which was Nolan's job. He never did it. There was no water to bathe in, so I smelled like the pigs. I had to fight on the school bus two to three times a week over smelling bad. The school knew we were hungry so they gave us breakfast in the mornings when we got to school. When I got home, I told them the school gave us breakfast, and I got a whipping for taking the food. They said to never take breakfast from the school again. So the next day they tried to give us breakfast, and we all refused. The schoolteacher kind of figured out what was going on, so she got me a job in the kitchen. She told them I had to work for my free lunch, so I got to eat my breakfast and lunch for a while.

One morning when we woke up, the grate had fallen out of the stove that we used to heat the house. I was just a small kid at the time. Nolan said we had to get a new stove. We got in the car and went to this gun club where they would have target practice. It was closed, of course. He put me through the window, and I unlocked the door. We loaded this stove into the trunk of his car; we stole it. While driving down the road, there was smoke still coming out of the stove. The stove was still warm from when the people had been there that day. So we took the stove home and hooked it up. Nolan then made my little brother and me walk across a cornfield—it probably wasn't far, but to a little kid it seemed like miles, and the snow was deep. We had to climb fences to get branches and wood, whatever we could carry for the stove. My brother would get cold and cry, so I would end up carrying all the wood and limbs back to the house.

Mom had gone to town for something—I don't remember what—and Nolan stayed home because there was a ball game on he wanted to see. The weather was really bad, almost like a blizzard, and the antenna was turning with the wind. So Nolan put me outside on a little roof so I would hold the antenna while he watched the ball game. My hands froze to the antenna pole. They must have fallen asleep because they woke up, wondered where I was, and found me on the roof. They told me never to tell anyone; I think they could have got in a lot of trouble. They poured water on my hands to get them unstuck from the pole. Then I went inside and put them in water. They soaked my hands and put me to bed. I still remember all night long my hands were burning, and I would tell them my hands were hurting. He would tell me I would be all right if I would go on to bed. So I did.

One Christmas day we didn't have a tree. He sent my brother and me across the fields to cut down a little tree. My brother almost froze to death coming back. I had to take him back home and then go back to get the tree.

I have seen Nolan get so mad that he would take pipe wrenches and knock the windows out of his car. He would kick us and hit us—it didn't matter with what because things didn't go his way. I have seen the times when my brothers and sister had to sit on a couch while the Simpson children ate. And like dogs, we would get the leftovers if there were any.

My cousin David Howland ran off with me one time because I couldn't take it anymore. I went to my dad's house. I told him they were beating us, and I didn't want to go back anymore. But he made me go back, and he drove us there. When he left, they beat us again. I was hit with a coffee cup; I was kicked and put in a corner for hours. The very next day my grandma stayed all night. I always thought this was so they wouldn't whip me anymore. My Uncle Dean came the next day too. Nolan came in cussing us cause he didn't know Dean was there, and Dean knocked him out the door. I never knew for sure, but I think it was because he was cussing at us kids.

Then they went and got Mom; naturally, she took up for Nolan. My grandma had gotten Dean off of Nolan.

One time when Stanley Green was there, we were all out in the front yard. Bobby Mootispaw and a few more people came over. They were all drunk, and I saw Stanley knock Bobby down. He hit the front end of a car that was on a jack and was going to stick it in his neck. I don't remember who got Stanley off of him, but that was an exciting time in life. We thought that was just it. I just couldn't get over Stanley going to pick that car up sit it on Bobby's neck.

My Uncle Shortie would come out. Winford was my aunt, who since has passed away. But anyway Shortie came over and brought us a bag of candy. He drank too, and Nolan never liked us talking to them cause they were Dad's family. But for some reason, when they came, he let us talk to them.

This is jumping back to the first part of the story. Back in the beginning, Dad on the weekends would give us money to go to the store. We would bring back candy, cookies and a pack of Camel non-filter cigarettes. I guess those where the times Mom and Dad were getting along. That was when they got the house on Paint Street, and my aunt and uncle lived upstairs with their kids Jo and Paul. I guess they didn't have much money. They didn't work; they didn't pay any rent. They lived there for years.

I can remember a time when my dad got into it with Buster. I don't know about what, but he chased him around the house with a hoe. He was going to hit him with it, but he didn't. They made up after that.

I can remember having a toy tractor that I pedaled and pulled a wagon behind it. My brother David was mean; he took my tractor and ran it over the hill. He hit the culvert and tore it all up. He begged me not to tell Dad or Mom, so I didn't. Then three weeks later, David stole Dad's truck; he was trying to drive it and wrecked at the same place where he tore up my tractor hitting the culvert. He tried to tell Dad someone else did it. Then David and Jo stole some guns from the Farm Bureau, which was a gun place in Greenfield, and my sister Sue saw them hide the guns in the attic. So the police came and asked my mom and dad if David had stolen anything and brought it here. They said no and my sister Sue said yes. She told them that he and Jo Penwell were putting stuff up the attic last night. So they found all the guns, and I think my parents had to pay for all of that. I'm not sure.

Mary Penwell was a good friend, and she lived on our street, Paint Street. On every holiday we would go to her house, or she would come to ours. We would all go to church; they would give me turkey. I would eat at our house, and then I would go to her house and eat with Henry, her son, and my friend. They would give me a big turkey leg cause I was so little, and they would take a picture cause I was so little. They thought that was funny.

Back when we lived on Route 41, I can remember one day that my brother Daniel was hungry. So he walked into the kitchen, took a biscuit, and hid it in his pocket. I will never forget this for the rest of my life. Nolan saw him eating the biscuit; he punched him in his nose and broke it. I tried to help him, but he knocked the hell out of me too. We were told never to tell Uncle Pete cause Pete would probably have killed him. I will never forget him doing that to that little boy for eating a biscuit.

Then there was my birthday. I hadn't seen my dad in a long time, a couple of years. Anyway, I ran into him; he asked me what I would like to have for my birthday. I said I wanted a bicycle. I had never had one, so he bought me a used bicycle that looked like new. So I took it home. And I don't know why, but Mom let me stay there for two days. Usually we weren't allowed to stay or even talk to him. But for some reason, she let me stay. When I got home, I got a whipping from Nolan. He was so jealous that he took a hacksaw and sawed my bicycle in half. Our friend Lauren Johnson asked what happened to my bicycle, and I said I didn't know; it just broke. He took it home and welded it. I always thought he knew what Nolan did.

It would be really cold, and we had no water or electricity. Instead, we had a potbelly stove and no wood. We also had very little coal; we even busted up furniture to make it. The well would freeze, and they would make me go out there in the middle of winter and prime that well. If I didn't bring any water back, I would get knocked down. So I tried my best to get that water. Sometimes I would get it, and sometimes I would not.

One day my cousin Buck and I were playing outside, and I stuck my hand underneath this car. I was piling dirt under the car, and he drove over my hand. I think my Uncle Pete was driving. Buck had told me to make a little dirt pile there. It scared Pete really bad. If it wasn't for Pete and Uncle Gary Smith, we probably would have never survived. I'm jumping around a little bit.

I don't know, but for some reason, we had to move from Route 41, and I thought that was going to be the happiest day of my life. They moved us to Greenfield on Baltimore Street. That's when hell really started; Nolan would whip us kids. He would put us in the corner for hours upon hours. There was a basement. He put Daniel in that basement one time with no lights. There was nothing; it was pitch black. It was an old, rock basement, and Daniel was screaming cause he didn't want to go in that basement. He punished him; then I would do something bad so I would go to the basement with him cause he was so afraid. I would tell Daniel it was alright. I was scared too, but I let on that I wasn't. I was four or five years older.

I remember that Pete had an old car that wouldn't run; he kept it in the garage on Baltimore. I would sneak in there and sleep. That's when he put that German police dog at the door, so I couldn't sleep in there anymore. The car was a Thunderbird, and I always wanted that car.

After the dog was killed, I would sneak girls in there when I'd see Nolan's car wasn't home. I had a girl in there one time, and Daniel caught me. He ran in the house and told Mom I was outside in the car beating this girl. I was stripped naked, and he thought I was beating her up. That was really funny, but Mom came outside; she was really going to beat the girl. My mom was really mean; she would fight anyone like a man. I talked her into not beating up the girl. She called me a little son of a bitch and all kind of good names for having that girl in the back seat of that car. But I don't think she minded that much. She just acted tough sometimes. But she never told Nolan about that girl. Then that girl would sit up there under that bridge for three weeks, and I couldn't get her to leave till finally she left. Then once in a while, my brother David and his wife Chee Chee would fight constantly. He took a hatchet and stuck in her head one night when they were fighting. Then she would do things to him; it was a real bad situation.

When I wanted to eat, I would go to Collin's Packing and steal lunch boxes from cars, and I finally went to jail. They sentenced me to permanent at the Ohio Youth Commission for being unruly. While I was in there, I never got a letter. I got one visit that I can remember, and they didn't even know I was there. I was sitting almost beside them. They didn't recognize me because it had been so long since they had seen me. So they asked someone where Roy was, and the old man I worked for—his name was Pop—said, "You don't even know what your own kid looks like? He is sitting right beside you."

That embarrassed them, which it should have. I didn't even look the same. It hurt my mother's feeling. She didn't want to leave me and she cried, but Nolan didn't give a damn. He was a hard-nosed son of a bitch. That was the only visit I ever had.

Back to being in jail, when I would get ready to go home, I'd run. There were three or four of us; we were deep in the woods in Sandusky Youth Camp—that's where I was sent. I was in there two years, I think— maybe a little longer. I got one letter from my grandmother. She told me she was dying, and my social worker wouldn't give me the letter. He read it to me, but he wouldn't let me have it. He was afraid I would run and threatened to put me in solitary, but I ran anyway. I ran lots of times, but they always found me and sent me back. Anyway, I made it home and told Grandma I was out. I didn't want to worry her; she was too ill. She told me to try to behave so I wouldn't have to go back, and I told her I would.

On those trips when I ran, I would stay with Doug Howland and hide behind his couch. I had a pillow and blanket, and Doug brought me food. His mom would bring Doug two or three hot dogs, and Doug would hand me some behind the couch. Then she would come back, and he would say he would really like a couple more. She would get them for him. Then I'd get caught, and they would send me back. Then I would run again.

One time, I ran and Doug didn't know I was behind the couch. His sister Bonnie did, but she had forgotten to tell Doug. The police came and knocked on the door, so Doug answered the door. They said they were looking for me because I had run again. They wondered if he knew where I was. Doug said no; he swore to God, which he hadn't. They asked if it was all right to search his house, so they could go about their business.

Doug said yes. Meanwhile Bonnie heard what he was saying. She came running down the steps saying no. They looked behind the couch; she was too late. They got me. To this day, he apologizes for me getting caught. He didn't know I was there; he would have never told on me. That's all right.

One time my brother and Jimmy Daugherty were in jail. David was hollering for me, so I went over and asked what he wanted. He wanted me to go get Mom or someone to get him out. In the meantime, they came and got me and Jack Daugherty. They had been looking for us too; we didn't know. They locked us up with them. In the meantime, we had this glue in our pockets; we had been sniffing glue. We went inside the cell sniffing glue, and Jimmy told on us. That's Jack's brother. He said we had glue that we had been sniffing, so they took the glue from us and sent me back again. So I was there again for about another year. I went back, and it was probably another year before I ran again.

Then one time, they called me to the office. My social worker and a couple were sitting there, and I thought about what could be wrong. They told me I couldn't get out cause I had never had a visit and no one ever wrote me a letter or anything like that. I had one visit and one letter in five years. So they sent me to a foster home, and I was there for a couple of years—I'm really not sure how long. They treated me really good, but I just didn't want to be there. I ate good, but they worked us hard; they worked us like dogs. It was a dairy farm, and we worked from daylight till dark.

At Christmastime, they would buy me a little more than the others, and as I look back on it, I think that their daughter liked me. But I wasn't smart enough to figure it out. All I could think about was going home. She would buy me watches, shirts, and pants; things that the other kids would get I was getting from her. But I just thought I was in jail, and these were the people guarding me.

They made me mad one time. I had saved up all my money and bought a pig; I only got fifty cents a day for working. When we were eating supper one evening, I asked him where my pig was; he said I was eating it. And I said I saved my money and bought that pig, but he went and had it butchered. I let it go, but I got even with him. I killed a cow and two or three calves, and I thought to myself that he had no right doing that to me. They called me into the house one day and asked if I killed the cow. I said no. They asked if I killed the calves. I said no.

Then he said, "If I give you the money back for the pig, will the cows quit dying?"

I said probably. So they gave me money and put it into a savings account.

Going back again to when I was in the juvenile detention center, I forgot that I knew Mr. Mathews; he was a black man. I had stabbed that boy with a fork, and Mr. Mathews would whip me and throw pool balls at me. He was a guard. When no one was around, he would say this was for whipping one of the brothers, he would mess me up pretty good. I never let on like I cared; I would stand there and take it like a man. Every time he would whip me, I would tell him he was still a nigger. I was mean at that time; I turned really mean. But they helped make me that way. One guard named Gary told Mr. Mathews that if he touched me again, he was going to whip him. And finally he ended up telling the warden what was going on. They asked me if he was whipping me, and I told them no, cause I didn't want to tell on anyone. I just wasn't going to snitch. He ended up getting fired. But until I left there, I told that other nigger whom I stabbed that if he messed with me, I would stab him again. He said if I left him alone, he would leave me alone. So I did.

When I first got there, I didn't talk to anyone. For six to seven months, I wouldn't even speak. But they put us in a holding cell once, and I saw Rick Simmons, who was my cousin, and he was crying. And I asked him what was wrong; he said they gave him six months. I told him if it made him feel any better, I had five years. And that relieved him. He thought six months wasn't so bad.

Then I ran away and they caught me. Hadley, the policeman in Greenfield, told me that my stepdad told on me. And that really broke my heart that they would do that to me, a family member. But he just didn't want us around. Never, till the day he died, did he want us around. So again, I was sent back to the foster home where I was at the time. They told me I was reaching the age of eighteen, and if I didn't run anymore, I would be released.

First, my brother David came to see me, and I told him I had been doing this for the last five years; I wanted to go home. So he said he would pick me up that night at the gas station. But in the meantime, he found out I was getting out, but I didn't know it. So he didn't come to pick me up, but I was there. Then came the guy who was watching us, Chester Collins. And I said I was just getting a can of pop. He asked where I got the money, and I said my brother. I told him I had lost it in the pop machine, but I really didn't. I just told him that so the next day they would give me fifty cents for the pop I didn't even try to get. And I wondered all day long why David treated me like that. He knew I was getting out, but I didn't.

So they released me. They were to pick me up at seven in the morning. Well seven o'clock came, ten o'clock came, twelve o'clock came, and so on. They told me they were going to have to put me back in jail for four months cause no one came after me. In four months I would turn eighteen, and then they could let me go. I told them I wouldn't run; they offered me a job if I would stay there and forget about going home. I still think it was about that girl, but I couldn't figure that out. I wanted to go home. I was stupid, I guess. All I could think about was going home. It was about twelve or one o'clock in the morning. They came beating on the door, and Chester said the people were there to pick me up. If I didn't want to go, I could just tell them to leave. Or if I changed my mind, I could come back.

On the way home, Nolan started lecturing me; he called me a little mother fucker and said he was going to cave my fucking brains in while hitting the ceiling of the car—that was his main thing. I kept thinking to myself, *Just wait till I get to Greenfield. You will never see me again.* He said I wasn't going to leave the house till I was eighteen.

When we got to Greenfield, he stopped at the gas station to use the bathroom. I told Mom I was going to get out right there, and she told me not to do that. She said to wait till he goes to bed and then just leave, if I wanted to leave. When we got right into Greenfield and stopped at the traffic light, David and Jimmy Daugherty were across the street at the filling station.

So I got out of the car, and Nolan said, "Don't you ever come to my house as long as you live."

I'll remember that till the day that I die. I thought, *What in the world? I haven't done anything to that son of a bitch.*

Anyway I didn't go back to his house. Then for some reason, he started talking to me. But anyway, I went with David and Jimmy that night. We got drunk, and I had a good time.

Back again to one of the other incidents when I ran off, I stayed in Pete's basement; Pete didn't even know I was there. It was a nasty basement; it was just hooked onto the side of the house like a cellar. I was there for about eight or nine months, and David would feed me. I'd sneak out at night and stay in the basement during the day. This girl named Pam Howland stayed there with me, and we ended up having a kid together. Her daddy made her get rid of the kid and said he was going to kill me. I couldn't blame him cause I got his daughter pregnant. And to this day, I've never seen this kid. He is probably pretty old by now; I don't know how old. Mom knows he was mine, and I don't know why they didn't try to see him. But I was in jail; they said I would never see him. But maybe some day I will.

Another time, we were hungry and I stole a semi. I could hardly drive it; I couldn't get out of first gear. I only drove it about two miles down into Felson Park. David and I took all this milk, cottage cheese, and stuff, and we just gave it away. Then they caught us. Pete had to pay back five or seven thousand dollars for that escapade. There was cheese, cottage cheese, chocolate milk, regular milk, butter, and all kind of things. He asked David L. how much milk we stole; David, he said, maybe two gallons. Then he handed him five dollars, and I knew then what was happening.

Then Pete said, "Just tell me the truth, and then you can go and shoot a couple games of pool."

So I started moving closer to the door. I knew Pete was getting ready to go off. David finally said we stole a whole semi, and I was right: Pete knocked him clear down.

Another time when we were hungry, I took Kenny Hess's car. They didn't have much to eat that day either, and I went to a little store in the country. We were going to rob them, so I took this chain. I hooked it around the bumper and around the store window. The window had bars on it. I pulled on that window, and the whole wall fell. So we robbed the store, and we were heading back home with all their food. That's all we usually took 'cause we were always hungry; they usually knew who robbed them 'cause I always took bologna and cheese. So we were heading back to Greenfield, and Coleman got after us—he was the policeman—so I shot down the road by Felsons Park.

I said, "David, we're gonna have to get out of the car cause there's another policeman coming down the street.

So I jumped and David didn't see it. The car was still moving so finally the car went underneath a light. David L. saw that no one was in the car but him, so he jumped. We got away, but Kenny Hess ended up in jail cause he wouldn't tell; he knew we had his car. They put him in the workhouse for thirty days. He never told on us, and I'm proud of him for that.

One time I recall that my Uncle Pete's boy and I went to a school function in Leesburg; we went to a dance. David L. got into a fight with one of those boys, and one of the boys got on top of him.

I went over and said, "You boys got him, so just leave him alone. You've whipped him; just let him up."

And he looked up at me and said, "When I'm done with him, I'm gonna whip your ass."

I told him that wasn't the answer I was looking for, so I reached into my pocket and cut his throat with a straight razor. The blood just ran down into my cousins' face, and I thought *God, I've killed him.*

But he didn't die; he survived. But if he had just let him go, I wouldn't have hurt him. His other mistake was when he said he was going to hurt me, cause then I wasn't afraid of anybody. Nothing ever came of me cutting that guys throat; I ran and hid from the law for a long time. They flew him away in a helicopter, and took him to Columbus. I saw him a few years later, and he told me he kind of deserved what he got. He knew I was known to carry a straight razor.

I said, "Then you were a little braver than I thought."

He tried to be my friend, but I knew he was trying to trick me into something, to get me somewhere and have someone hurt me. So I just told him to stay away from me, and I would stay away from him. It worked out better that way.

My other cousin Paul Dorman and I had nowhere to go. We kind of lived on the street, in the pool hall doors, and in cars. We ran women and got drunk. We would go into the Diamond Grill that was across the street; that is the roughest bar I have ever been in. There was a fight every single day and night in that bar. In there they would play for keeps; they would try to put you to sleep. One Fillmore boy shot another guy over his false teeth. Fillmore broke his false teeth when he hit him in the mouth, so the guy went outside, got a shotgun, and blew him clear out the window. But it didn't kill him. But to this day—and its was twenty-five or thirty years ago—that guy's still in church. I was just walking into the bar, and Frank came flying out the window. It was the wrong place to be; don't bring a knife to a gun fight. Well, I went back down the street to the other bar and told them what was going on down there. Before I knew it, there were 10,000 policemen. As I looked back, I was homeless cause I had no place to go. We took blankets off clotheslines to keep warm at night and would steal clothes when we could find them.

Another time in the Diamond Grill—while I'm thinking about this—I got into a fight, and that's when I cut that man's throat. I had to go out to my Dad's in California. And I lived out there a year or two because I hurt that guy pretty badly.

I used to run in the bars. I was around eighteen years old; I used to run with my friend Johnny Jackman. Johnny was probably fifteen or sixteen years older than I was, and he took care of me a little bit. Johnny and I used to go and fight all the time. We used to go to the Emerald Inn and a couple other bars in Washington Courthouse We would fight every weekend. We would tell ourselves we weren't going to fight on the way to Washington, but we knew in the back of our minds that we were going to fight someone.

We would take my cousin Buck with us, and he would get so drunk that we couldn't understand a thing he said. People were afraid of him. I can remember one night we were sitting at the Emerald Inn, and this big guy— he was probably 6' 2" or 6' 3"; a pretty big fella—kept writing me notes. I couldn't read very well, so I handed them to Johnny and asked him what they said.

Johnny looked at me and said, "Hell, he's going to kill you."

So automatically, I pulled my knife out; he had a trachea in his throat, a hole in his throat where he could breath or something. I remember I stuck that knife right in that hole and raised him up out of that chair. I had blood running down my arm.

Johnny kept saying, "Please. Don't kill him."

So I let him go. I thought he was going to hurt me cause I was little, a lot smaller than him. But looking back at it, that's not the way it's to be done.

Another time we were in Greenfield at Johnny's Bar. Some guys from Portsmouth or Knockemstiff started trouble, so I picked up a chair and hit the guy over the head with it. I would have liked to have killed him, and Johnny was fighting the other guy. But they came in there for trouble. Every time those boys came out there, they would come for trouble.

But like I said before about the Diamond Grill, it wouldn't matter who you were, where you came from, or how mean you were; the people there would hurt you. If you had a chip on your shoulder, someone would knock it off. They were some crazy people in a very small town.

Another time we were in the bar, David L., Uncle Pete, and I. My Uncle Pete got into a fight with this great big guy, and David L. and I went out back and hid cause we were going to help Pete.

We had a can of mace, and I told David L., "I'm going to see if this mace works before I shoot that guy in the face with it."

I sprayed myself and David L. right in the face with it, so we didn't get to help Pete. As it turned out, he didn't need any help anyway. We couldn't see for a couple of hours.

There are a lot of things I can't tell or put in the tape or the book, cause I might go to prison over them.

One day Danny Pryor and I were standing in the Diamond Grill. We were getting ready to go to the show. He had his wife and I had my wife. This drunk came out the back door said something really nasty to us, and I beat this man almost to death. I had to go to the doctor to get my rings pulled out of my fingers. I beat him in the face so much. That man didn't deserve that whipping for what he said, but I was just crazy. I guess I didn't have anywhere to go; I was kind of a street person, I guess.

I can recall my Uncle Gary, who is my dad's brother. He took care of me for years. If it wasn't for him, I probably would have starved to death. Even when I was married to my first wife Shirley, he was there for me and took care of us. He helped Mom out for years because Dad left us. But you couldn't much blame him. Gary and I ran around a lot drinking beer. We were heading home one night at about 2:30 AM. They were doing construction, and they had the road closed.

Gary said, "You can't go that way, Roy. The road is closed."

I said, "You dumbass, we're not driving; we're walking."

So I went around the barricade, fell clear off a hill, and broke my leg.

He looked at me and said, "I told you we can't go that way."

My first wife Shirley was crazy; she was insanely jealous. She would think I was running women when I really wasn't at first, and I told her one day, "You keep bringing it up that I'm running women, and I'm going to start."

She never stopped, so I started. One of my best friends Ralph Brust stayed with me a lot cause he had no place to go. We were out drinking for a couple of days. I came home and finally got back in the house. She finally stopped her arguing and was fixing breakfast. I got up to go to the bathroom. Ralph looked up at me and said, "Roy, your underwear is on inside out, and you have them on backwards."

Well, to make a long story short, she threw me out of the house.

I said, "Ralph, you know it's cold and raining. Why couldn't you keep your mouth shut about the underwear?"

He knew who I was with cause he was with me.

Another time I was with my friend Jack Dourghty, my cousin Rowdy Green, and Jimmy Dourghty. We were riding around drinking beer, and they made me mad. I pulled this gun out and I told this guy in the back seat—he was a Calhoun—that was going to kill him. So I shot at him a couple of times, and thank God, I missed. They probably would have put me away for life with my reputation. I don't even remember what that argument was about. I remember Jack giving me the gun. Jack and I ran around together for years and years. We were really good friends.

Another good friend of mine was Rick. We were out to the drive-in, and he went after some popcorn or something. I heard a commotion going on up there, so I went to see what it was. Rick had a corn knife, and I had a hunting knife. There were probably seventy-five blacks, and it all started the week before when this black guy and Rick got into it. The black guy called him a honky, and he called him a nigger. Then the fight broke out there, but they didn't whip us. They were scared of us. They knew that if someone walked into those knives, someone was going to die. We finally got away; the Highland County sheriff came, and Ross County police came. There were cops everywhere looking for us because we had done other things.

Rick and I were really good friends. I was with him till the day he died. We were out with these girls; we were drinking beer and thought we would ride to Bainbridge. That's the day Rick died. He went around a curve and hit a tree. He was underneath the truck and was moaning. I tried to help him, but I couldn't. I got the girls out of there, but the truck was leaking gas really badly. When the Life Squad got there, he was dead. They opened an investigation on me because they thought I killed him, but I didn't. They spent two or three thousand dollars trying to see if I killed him, but I didn't kill him.

Speaking of killing, my family is pretty crazy, the whole bunch of them. I don't know one male member who hasn't been in prison for hurting someone. It has been going on for generations. That's why I moved my family away from them, hoping they wouldn't follow that path. And so far—knock on wood—they haven't.

After I got married, I thought things would change, and I would stop being so mean. But I wasn't. I had my first daughter, Utalcia; my Aunt Edna delivered her at the hospital. The doctor was late.

She kept telling the nurse, "Here comes the baby."

They kept saying, "We're going after the doctor."

By the time they got back, my aunt had delivered the baby. That was something Edna talked about till she died.

Then we had David, and he slept with me. We never slept with his mother much because she wanted to fight all the time. Then Davey and I had our own little room on the couch.

Then I recall having Stacy; she is the one kid I won't forget because on the way to the delivery room, I had to stop and have a fight. My brother Daniel was in the alley fighting with these men, and I stopped.

I can remember Shirley saying, "The baby is coming."

I said, "Just hold on five minutes."

So I had to fight, and it seemed like I fought forever—but I know we didn't. We were riding up the road, and my shirt was all ripped. Mom was in the back seat cussing the guys who were fighting, and my wife was in the front seat having a baby. If you don't think that wasn't exciting, we made it to the hospital in time, but just in time.

I can remember slowing down a little bit after Stacy, and I was working for Bobby Roberts. Every Friday Nolan and the rest would come and try to get money from me cause they wouldn't work. If I bought a pack of diapers for one of my kids, I'd have to buy two packs, or my baby wouldn't get any diapers. If I bought a loaf of bread, I had to buy two loaves. When I'd buy groceries, I would go in the front door, and they went right out the back door cause Shirley was afraid of them. I had to tell them to stay the hell away from the house; I wasn't going to feed them all. But that didn't work.

My first wife would never leave me alone. She always thought I was running women, but—honest to God—at first, I wasn't. I never messed with a woman; I was happy at first. But she was so crazy about me running women that I started to. If I was going to be accused all the time, I decided I might as well go for it. That was my theory about it. I left one day, and I came back. I wasn't with a woman that day, but she took all my clothes, put them in a trash sack, and left them outside. In the meantime, the trashman came; he took my clothes, and all I had on was my pajamas, a top, and a pair of house slippers, flip-flops.

She said, "You'll not go to town now, will ya?"

So I got in the little car, went downtown to the bar, and walked in there in my pajamas and flip-flops. My feet were frozen, but I just wanted to show her that I'd go anyway. Finally Mom had to go get me some clothes cause I didn't have anything.

There was another time when we lived with my sister Sue and Kenny Hess up above an apartment house on Jefferson Street. A roach crawled into my ear. I let it go for a couple days. I finally went to the hospital because I didn't know what was wrong. They said a roach had crawled in my ear, and they had to pull it out of there. What happened was that I went to my dad's in London, and my whole face had swelled up. He took me over there; that was when they pulled it out.

If it weren't for my brother-in-law and my sister Sue, I wouldn't have even made it sometimes even before we got married. They would help me.

I remember one time when I was drinking beer and partying, we lived up above a bar. This guy was staying all night with us, and he wouldn't shut up. I told him to turn the TV off and just shut up, but he wouldn't shut up. So I got out of bed. I was in a two-story apartment, and there was a fight downstairs. The police was already down there, and I threw Steve out the window. He landed on the police cruiser; that got me a year in jail. But it didn't hurt him that badly.

Another time, Shirley wouldn't shut up about getting the dog's tail cut off; it was a poodle. I was half drunk, and she kept wanting me to take that dog to the vet to get its tail cut off. We didn't really have the money, so I grabbed the hatchet, laid the dog down, and cut its tail.

I handed her the dog and said, "There. All of the dog's tail is gone."

I probably cut it a little shorter than I was supposed to cut it.

I remember another time when I was in Naples, Florida with a friend, Leroy Perdon, and his stepson, Clyde. I went to the bar, a place called The Back Door. We were shooting pool, and somehow Clyde said something to some black guys that caused an awful fight. So I had a meat cleaver in my car—it was a rather large meat cleaver; it was from Collin's Meat Packing Company. It weighed about 115 to 120 pounds.

I went into that bar cause I had to help fight these guys; they surrounded us. So there happened to be a guy from my hometown who knew me; he was a black guy whose name was Stagal. That one black guy was standing there, and he told that other black guy to just charge me and take that meat cleaver. The other black guy said, "He will chop your head off. I know him."

And he was right. I was going to kill him. Then I had to call Leroy or have somebody call; Leroy came and got us. He couldn't get us out of there without pulling a pistol, and that was all over Clyde. He was someone who couldn't whip himself out of a wet paper bag.

Leroy used to pay me a hundred dollars a day just to watch Clyde so he wouldn't get hurt or anything. He drank a lot. I didn't keep that job long. I am jumping around a little bit, but I can't help it. I am trying not to do so.

When I got into it with that guy and ran off to California, we lived in a little town called Taft. I hid out in the desert for a long time till things cooled down. At least I thought they did, so I got on a plane and flew back home. It wasn't but a short time later when they arrested me for assault. I was facing twenty-five to fifty-five years. That was assault with a deadly weapon. But my Uncle Pete was known to have really good lawyers; he bought me a lawyer and got me out of that trouble.

I had an attorney out of Cincinnati. His name was Eugene Smith. He was a black man, but he was very smart. He was a criminal lawyer. We used him a lot. I have been arrested probably fifty-seven times or sixty times; most of them were for violence, drunkenness, and fighting.

I had a friend, Johnny Jackman; he ran the Diamond Grill Bar. That's where all the trouble was, and we used to go to Washington Courthouse just to get away from there for a while.

We were drinking beer one day, and this guy couldn't talk. He had a hole in his throat; he had something wrong with him. I guess and he was a pretty big man, and he kept writing letters and notes to me. I couldn't read very well, so I asked Johnny to tell me what they said. He said he was going to kill me, so I pulled out my knife and stuck it into that hole in his throat out of which he was breathing. He stood up, and blood was running out of the hole and down my arm. Johnny grabbed me. That was just one of the stupid things I used to do. If it wasn't for Johnny, I probably would have killed him.

Two or three weeks later, we were back in Greenfield in a bar, and this guy and I got into it. He pulled a gun out on me, and I pulled out a knife. I was charging him, and he had the gun. That was really stupid.

When my brother killed that man, he was in jail in Washington Courthouse. He wanted me to slip him a hacksaw blade to get him out cause the window was on the side. I was going to do it. I went there that evening to give it to him, but they had already transported him. That probably was a good thing because he probably would have died. They would have shot him.

I used to sneak into my mother's house when my stepdad would leave to visit her and maybe grab a sandwich. They would see him coming and they would tell us to run. I would go out the back door, so he wouldn't see us. I didn't want to cause my mom problems. He bought this German police dog to guard the garage too. I couldn't sneak in there and sleep; the dog bit my sister Bonnie in the neck. The very next day they found that dog hanging on the clothesline with its throat cut. My brother David did that because that dog bit my sister.

One time, I got arrested on Baltimore Street; I think I was twelve or thirteen years old. The judge sent me away to permanent confinement with the youth commission. They came and got me at my mom's house, and I didn't see them for five years, except for when I ran from that jail. There's a lot of things I just can't talk about. I could probably be in a lot of serious trouble for those things.

When I would run from that jail, they couldn't find me. There was a place in Greenfield called the Stone Quarry where everyone used to swim; that's where I used to bathe, and sometimes I would sleep down there.

When I was in the sixth grade at the Greenfield School, my school-teacher, Mrs. Priest, was really nice to me, and we got along really well. When I would get into trouble, she would try to get me out of it. If the teacher down the hall came for me, she wouldn't let him; she would tell him to mind to his own class. She would put me in the hallway for being mean; if he got me, she told him to mind his own business and put me back in class. She wouldn't let him paddle me.

If I'm not wrong, that was when we met the Hess family—Kenny and his family—and now he is my brother-in-law. I went with his sister off and on from the sixth grade till I was about eighteen or nineteen. Her family didn't want me around because of the things I used to do. I was so mean; I'd fight. So David tried to keep us away, but he couldn't do it. Then one day, her sister came from up north and picked her up; I haven't seen her in thirty years. That's another story.

After Debbie came and got Teresa, I got a hold of my dad.

A week or so after that, I cut a man's throat in the Diamond Grill. We were shooting pool for a beer; at the time, beer was about fifty cents, which was nothing.

I beat this old hillbilly in a game of pool, and I told him, "I'll have a Miller."

One word led to another, and he said he wasn't going to buy me a beer. He hit me, and he knocked me under the pool table. Then he reached under there to get me. I cut his throat. As he grabbed his neck and was running, I was chasing after him and cut the whole back end out of his pants. I don't know how many, but he had a lot of stitches in his neck and his ass. A cop named Dizzy told me that. He said that I had hurt that guy pretty badly, and that I'd better go away for a while, till I could see what happened.

So I got a hold of my dad. He was in California at the time, and his girl-friend lived in Springfield. So I stayed with her for a couple days till Dad sent me money and a bus ticket. I went to California and stayed for about a year or so. Dad got me a job at the mine where he was working; they made cat litter. I worked there for six or seven months—I'm not sure how long. It was a good time out there; I had a good time. I had plenty of money; I don't know why I didn't stay. I missed Greenfield and I don't know why. It was always nothing but trouble for me in Greenfield. And while I was out there, I had a car. Dad got me a car. I had plenty of money and new clothes; we went places and ate out. I think that was the first time I had a big dinner in my life. We went out to eat, and I think it cost Dad about $80.00.

I thought, *My God, that's a lot of money to pay for one meal.*

And as life went on, I realized that was about normal.

And as time went on, I told Dad I wanted to go home. I was getting homesick, so instead of riding the bus, he put me on a plane. It was a 747. It was the first time I was ever on a plane. He bought insurance on me, just in case the plane wrecked.

I told him, "You know that plane's going to fall."

He thought that was funny, and he laughed.

I got into Dayton, Ohio. I called my mother and asked her if she would come and get me cause I had no way home. She said the only way Nolan would come and get me was if I paid $30.00 or $40.00. I told them okay, just to get home. On the way home to Greenfield, all he talked about was my dad and how much he hated him. I couldn't help it. I hated Nolan so I just let him run his mouth. Mom just said to shut up and let him run his mouth. But as we down the road, how much I hated him. I think he was the one who made us so mean. I really do cause of the way he treated us.

And when I got back to Greenfield, I thought it was all over about me cutting that man's throat, but it wasn't long before they arrested me. They were talking about twenty-five to thirty-five years in prison for what I did. My Uncle Pete got me a lawyer, and we went to court; this guy I cut was a hillbilly boy who was not very bright. He looked over to his dad, and he even thought the prosecutor was my lawyer.

He said, "Look at all the lawyers Roy's got."

My lawyer nudged me not to say anything cause he wanted everyone to think they were all my lawyers, and no one was on his side. It worked. He got up there, and the judge asked him what I had done to him. He said I cut him, and my lawyer asked him how many beers he had. He went from a six-pack to eighteen beers.

My lawyer asked him, "Are you a farmer?"

He said yes.

He said, "Do you work around heavy equipment?"

He said yes.

"Is there anyway you could have hurt yourself on any of that equipment?"

He said yes, and the judge put the gavel down.

He said, "This case is dismissed."

My attorney tricked him into thinking he cut himself on his tractor. And he keep saying, "But I didn't. He did it."

And it didn't do any good. He hung himself.

Back to the sixth grade, I skipped school a lot, and I was probably around twelve years old or so. I was still in Mrs. Priest's room because I wasn't learning anything, but now I wished I would have. We would take these little girls into David L.'s basement or garage, and finally the school got wind of it. Finally Mrs. Priest sat me down and had a long conversation with me about it. She said I might get one of these little girls pregnant or whatever. To make a long story short, we had a different girl skipping school with us every day.

Sitting here today thinking about all these things that I have done and that have happened to me, it's a wonder I'm still alive or not in prison for life.

When I got back from California and after court and all, I got to running the bars again. I was around nineteen or twenty, I guess. That's when I met the kids' mother. I met her, and we ran around for about four or five months. We ended up getting married, and she was really mean to me. She was so jealous and I don't know why because at first, I wasn't doing anything; there were no women. I'd look at them, but that was as far as it went. I wasn't running women, but every day she would say I was running a woman. Even if one would be on TV, she would say I wanted that woman, and handsome I was not. At least I didn't think so.

After a couple of years, we had our first daughter, Utalcia, and I thought the world of her. I bought her toys she couldn't even ride for the first two years. We stayed with Sue and Kenny, my sister and brother-in-law, a lot cause we didn't have anywhere to go. There wasn't much work down there. But at the time, I probably didn't want to work anyway cause I was raised that way.

I can remember when Talcia was born, I was there with my Aunt Edna. We were in Washington Courthouse Hospital, and they told Edna she couldn't stay.

She said, "I'm her mother," cause Shirley's family never showed up anyway. I don't think they liked me very much.

Shirley had a hard time having the baby; she was in labor for hours. Edna was screaming, and I went in to see what was wrong.

She said, "Get someone. The baby is coming." She kept saying, "Here comes this baby. What do I do? Get someone."

So Edna really delivered that baby; there was no doctor or nurse, just Edna and me. Then she went out into the hallway and almost passed out. I thought that was so funny. Till the day old Edna died, she thought about that. Utalcia was the first baby she ever delivered.

Then we had David a short time after that, and I was working, I think, at that time for the Roberts Construction, off and on. Then every Friday, when I would get paid, there would sit Nolan wanting money. I didn't even live with them, but I gave them money because I knew they didn't have anything to eat most of the time. I think I worked for Bobby for a couple years.

Then came Stacy, who is my youngest. We went down to borrow my Uncle Pete's car—cause mine was broken—to get Shirley to the hospital, cause with her pregnancies, it took a long time. I thought we had plenty of time to get there. My mother was with me, and I was driving down Jefferson Street. I went down an alley to get away from the traffic to get on 41 and to Washington Courthouse, and there was my brother Daniel. He was in a fight. I mean, there were four or five guys; they were all fighting. My mom said to stop and help him, so I stopped.

Shirley was screaming in the back, "The baby's coming."

I told her, "You're just going to have to hold on one minute."

So I got outside; we fought for five or ten minutes helping my brother. It seemed like forever, but it wasn't.

I told him, "Shirley's having a baby."

He said, "Nobody asked you to stop. Help me."

I don't think he understood that I couldn't deliver a baby. We were fighting those boys. Someone threw a bottle and it cracked Uncle Pete's windshield. I knew I was going to be in trouble with him. So when I got back to Greenfield with the car, he already knew what had happened. I don't know who told him; he thought it was funny. I told him I would pay for the windshield, but Pete had a lot of money. He just laughed it off.

He said, "I'll fix the windshield. Don't worry about it." I really appreciated that.

At that time, I was tired of Shirley telling me I was running women, which I wasn't. So finally I started running women. She was telling me every day I was, and I told her if it didn't stop, I was going to start. So I figured why not do it if I was getting accused every day, so I did. I was about twenty-one or twenty-two.

I started running around with my Uncle Gary. I loved that little man; he was so good to me. He paid my electric bill when I needed it and bought food. I don't know what I would have done without him.

Anyway, every Friday and Saturday, I would get with him and drink because I didn't have any money and he would buy me drinks. We would take the barroom women up to his house at night after the bars closed. His wife had passed away years before in a car crash; she was hit by a drunk driver. He never did get over that. I would never get over it either. Gary had a perfect life with her; they never argued. He really loved that woman.

Anyway, we would get these old whores, and we would take them up to Gary's house. Shirley would come looking for me, and she could never find me. This went on for years. Then my dad stayed with me off and on, and Dad said he could hear Shirley cussing me. We were down the road about a half mile.

He asked me, "Why do you stay with that women?"

I told him, "I stay with her because of my children."

I didn't want to break up the family. But at that time, I had two or three girlfriends. I'd run around, going to Danny Prior's and go out to the circle with the women, and Shirley never could find me. Then I would go home after staying out for two or three days.

I can recall one time when Ralph and I were out drinking for a couple days; I told him, "You know we're out of money, so let's just go home."

He said okay; he lived with us. I was lying on the couch, and I got up to go to the bathroom. He looked at Shirley; I had my underwear on inside out and backwards. She was frying eggs and bacon, and she threw them clear across the floor.

So I grabbed my hat and my pants, went out the door, and said, "Ralph, why did you tell on me?"

He said, "I don't know. I didn't mean to."

To make a long story short, I had to go to Mom's house to lay low.

Sue and Kenny moved to Cincinnati, so I just thought I would move to Cincinnati and quit my drinking, which I did. Dad moved up there with us. We lived in a trailer on Nine-Mile Road; we stayed for probably a year and went right back to Greenfield. It's just like a magnet. It's like I couldn't get rid of Greenfield. Everywhere I would go, I would end up back there. And I don't know why, because there was nothing there for me but trouble. And then Sue and Kenny moved back too, right after I did. They were living in an apartment over the gas station called Jonco. I asked Kenny if I could stay for a couple days; I laid down and a roach crawled into my ear. I didn't know what happened, but my ear started swelling. Dad was in London, Ohio, and he asked me to come there and get a job. So I said okay. So I went to London and started working. My ear kept hurting, and it was swollen to double its size, as was the side of my face. I told Dad something was wrong. So Dad took me over to the emergency room. They stuck something down in my ear, and they pulled this roach out of my ear. I was very embarrassed. They put medicine in my ear, and after a few days, I was back to normal. The doctor said it was the first roach he ever pulled out of someone's ear. I didn't really want to talk to him about it because I was so embarrassed. We stayed up there with Dad for three or four months; then it was right back to Greenfield. I rented an apartment, and we stayed there for two or three years. Things weren't getting better. Shirley was still obsessed, wouldn't leave me alone, and always thought I was running women. At this time, I was because I got tired of her saying I was running women when I wasn't.

I can remember Shirley and I went up to my Mom's; it was around Christmastime. They didn't have a tree or any food cause Nolan would take the money and go to Kentucky or Florida every time he got a dollar. So I went and bought them a tree and a turkey. After a couple of hours, I went back, and Nolan had taken the tree and thrown it out the door. The dogs were eating the turkey.

I said, "Mom, I just spent all my money buying you a turkey and a tree. Why did you let him do that?"

But I think she loved him more than life itself, even after the way he treated us Bennett kids—God only knows what we went through. I can remember Baltimore Street, before I got sent away—I'm jumping around again—he would put us in a corner and put apples on our heads. I was probably eleven or twelve; I don't know.

I woke up one morning, and David had put an artificial apple on my head. He was shooting it off with a 22 rifle, but I think he was so damn dumb that if I had risen up, he would have killed me.

So the next day, I got him back. There was a set of steps where we slept right there in the hallway. There wasn't enough room, so David and I had to sleep together. Daniel and David were asleep, and Gary came down the steps. If you didn't do what Gary wanted you to do, he would start screaming and Nolan would come and he just start punching you, because you were just his slave, I guess. Anyway, Gary said he had to pee, and I talked him into peeing on David's head. I thought that was really funny.

After that judge sent me away, I was living on Baltimore Street. That was the last time I got to see them for years. The parole officer came to get me that same day to take me to the Ohio Youth Commission, and Nolan thought that was funny. I was so scared, but I never showed it. I never let on that I was scared, but I was really scared. I looked back because the parole officer was scared of me; he was just a little old man. So he hand-cuffed me to the seat, and I looked back to see if someone would be there to wave good-bye. Daniel was the only one there, and I think it bothered him a little bit. Neither my mother nor anyone else was there to wave good-bye to me. I also didn't realize I was going to be there for four or five years.

It was almost five years. But while I was gone, Bonnie, Daniel, and Georgie were still getting beaten daily. My cousin Michael Green told me Daniel would go to school and his legs and his back where he was beaten with a switch would be so bloody he couldn't even take gym class. Michael said he was going to tell one time, but he didn't. I wished he would have.

My youngest was only a baby at this time, and I think I was drinking pretty heavily. Shirley and I were having problems, and I think, at this point in my life, I was running women, drinking, and fighting. Those were the things to do at the Diamond Grill. Buck, my cousin, got in a fight with this guy; he pulled a gun on us and was going to shoot us. Buck stepped in front of me—I was drunk and he was drunk too—and I stepped in front of Buck. I pushed him and he pushed me, and the guy thought we were crazy.

I said, "Let him shoot me."

Buck said, "No, let him shoot me."

The guy got scared and ran, which was really stupid now that I look back at it. At the time, we thought it was really funny, but it wasn't—he was the one with the gun.

Another night Leroy Purdon came up from Florida. He lived in Naples, and he would come to the town of Greenfield to visit us. We all got to drinking, and Leroy was really huge man, probably 600 pounds. Well he went home with me that night, and we didn't have much to eat cause we hadn't been to the store. I was drunk and Leroy was drunk, and he just wouldn't shut up about something to eat. I told him we had to wait till the store opened up. I couldn't thaw anything cause I didn't have a microwave or anything then. I looked outside and Shirley had two white rabbits. Leroy fell asleep and I went outside and knocked those rabbits in the head. I fried them up for me and Leroy cause he was really hungry; but that wasn't good when Shirley woke up because we ate her rabbits. She really got mad.

Then my Uncle Pete was running dope really bad and went to Florida one time. He asked me if I would watch his house. When I was watching his house, the police raided it, but they didn't find anything. I was kind of glad cause they would probably have arrested me.

At this time Shirley and I were really struggling about where to live because I was drinking more than I was working. My Uncle Gary Smith used to help me pay my bills and buy food. On Sundays, we used to go to my Uncle Jake and Aunt Joyce's to eat dinner with them, and Jake and I would drink beer. Shirley and I lived up on South Street and Daniel and Tangy, my brother and his wife, were living with us. Shirley and I were arguing pretty good at this time, and I told her not to ever set my clothes out again. Cause I would never come back. So I came home one night, and there were my clothes. I put them in my car and said I was going to leave and was not coming back. We argued constantly. It wasn't good. So I went down to the bar, and I sat down drinking a beer. I was thinking about going to Cincinnati to find my old girlfriend. I didn't know if she was married or what the deal was; I was just going to give it a shot. Then I got to drinking, and finally I talked Darlene into going out with me. I told her I was much older than I was. I lied to her. It was her birthday, and she finally agreed to go out with me. So the next day, after we drank that night, I didn't want to leave anymore; I wanted to be with her, but I wasn't sure whether she did or not. I talked to her, and she started going with me.

We met on August 9, 1982.

I was staying with my Uncle Gary most of the time after I left Shirley, and she was still trying to get me to come home. I just made my mind up that it was over. It just wasn't working. So one night, Darlene stayed all night with me at my Uncle Gary's, and Shirley pulled up and headed for the house. Darlene went into the bathroom, and Shirley came in and walked through the house. Gary's girlfriend told her it was Darlene, but it wasn't like she didn't know it cause I told her. Every day she would try to get me to come back to her. I knew if I did, it would be the same thing over and over. I knew it was just time to quit.

So finally Darlene and I moved in together; well, we didn't really move in together. We were out one night, and I was working for a friend of mine, Bob Montie. We used to work on washers and dryers; I was helping him a little bit to make some extra money. And while I was out, Shirley took my kids to Darlene's and had my sister Lisa drop them off.

To make a long story short, they never went back to Shirley. I kept them. When she dropped them off, I didn't know whether Darlene would want them or not, but if she didn't, I would have headed to my sister's. That's where I used to go every time I had a problem; I don't know why.

But Darlene and I went from there to Washington Courthouse, and Shirley hadn't seen the kids in probably close to a year. Darlene and I were still drinking on the weekends, and Leigh Ann used to watch the kids and take care of them while we were gone.

Darlene and I were out drinking one night with some friends. We were out to the creek, and someone stole Darlene's purse. That really made me mad.

So I just walked up through all those guys, and I said, "I don't know which one of you took her purse, but if it's not back at our house tomorrow, I'm going to find everyone of you."

The next morning Darlene said someone knocked on the door and handed her the purse with nothing missing. I don't know if they were afraid of me or what. I had told them what the consequences were going to be if they didn't return the purse. Everybody out there knew me, and they knew I meant what I said.

At this time, Darlene and I were really close. We went together everywhere and did a lot. At that time she found out my real age; I don't think she was very happy about it, but we just stuck together. We had it pretty rough: We had these five kids at home; she was working at the shoe factory, and I was getting disability. Shirley wasn't giving me any money—nothing—

and neither was her ex-husband, Bob. It was really hard. But we never went hungry and never went without. I would see to that. If we would run low on money or food, I would go take it from somebody. I have killed pigs in a field and butchered them; I had killed cattle, take half the beef, and run with it. They never knew where it came from.

Then we had to put up with Rome Poole about every day, and Darlene didn't like that a bit. He used to get drunk and come to our house. He wanted to drink beer all hours of the night, but Darlene had to work. So we didn't let that go on too long.

The kids would get to crying cause they wanted to see their mother, but she wouldn't come and see them. We lived in Washington at that time. So I went to hunt for her, and I found her. I tried to convince her to see the kids, and all she wanted to talk about was getting with me. I told her that was never going to happen again. So she just wouldn't visit her children.

But I tried to get along with everybody for the kid's sake cause they didn't ask for this. But it sure would have been a big help if the other parents would have helped us.

And at this time, I was still really jealous of Darlene, and I got mad one time. I ran my fist through the fish tank and cut myself up pretty badly. I had to go to the hospital to get stitches, and I don't know why I did that. It was probably the beer and my past history of violence.

Another time Darlene and I were out drinking with Uncle Gary. We were all drunk, and we drove this car up the road on McClain at probably 100 miles an hour. We didn't stop at any stop signs or anything. We went down to Gary's house and talked Darlene into making eggs and bacon. I tried to be a smartass with Darlene, and after she made the eggs and bacon—I was still drinking beer, and so was Gary—I told her I didn't want any, so she put the bacon and eggs on the plate and sat it on the table. I told her again I didn't want any, and she pushed that plate of eggs and bacon onto my lap. Gary thought that was the funniest thing; he laughed and laughed over that. There I was with eggs and bacon all over me. I was really mad; it took me awhile to get over it.

My mother really liked Darlene. My mother was the one who introduced me to Darlene. I told my mom I'd like to go out with her, but she probably wouldn't. And she laughed.

We were still up in Washington Courthouse, and we finally got this house to rent from Whitie Ward on Haney Lane. I didn't know if Darlene and I were really going to make it. Her friends didn't want her around me, and I was so jealous. I didn't know if it was going to work or not. I think I was trying to be more protective than anything. Her friend told her she should leave me. All I wanted to do was fight; I was violent, which was really bad.

So we moved to a house in the country; it had eighty-eight acres. He only charged one hundred dollars a month. I thought that was really cheap;

we had all those kids and didn't have much money. So we rented it; they were the best renters I ever had in my life. They would clean their freezer and bring fruit and vegetables to us. Whitey would go up on the hill and cut wood, and he would drop us off a truckload about every week. He would stop, have a beer with us, and sit to bullshit for a little bit.

I used to take care of his son Maynard Ward. Maynard was an alcoholic and had been for years. He lived just up the road from us, within walking distance. His family owned his property too. We always had Ralph Brust with us; he was a friend I had had for a long time. I would make him work cutting wood to help feed him. Then I would take him home. I think those kids had a good time down there on that hill.

One time it was December, and it was really warm. Darlene, the kids, and I were there that day, and I thought we ought to cook out. These Muspaughs pulled up, so I went over there to see what they wanted. They were drunk and they wanted a beer. I had twelve, so I gave them six of my beers.

I told them, "My kids are here, so you're just going to have to leave."

They started getting rowdy, so I told my stepson Bobby to go get Maynard to help me 'cause there were three of them. I had my knucks in my back pocket; I used to pack them everywhere I went. One got out of the car, and he spit on me. God be my judge, I don't hardly remember anything after that. I took them knucks, and I beat him almost to death. The other one pulled a knife on me, and I took his knife from him and whipped all three of them. I don't know how I did that to this day, and the kids were screaming cause they had never seen anything like that before. All I could think about was they were going to hurt the kids. So I whipped them and put them back in the car.

Maynard and Bobby were coming up the road, and Maynard said, "I thought you needed help."

I said, "I got it under control, but thanks for coming to help."

And Bobby was going to help me too, bless his heart, but after that, things started to change for me. I didn't want my kids to see me fighting, and I didn't want them to grow up like I had grown up. So I started rethinking things a little bit.

One time, Bobby, Rome Poole, and I went to the bar called Furmans, and we were sitting there drinking a beer. Bobby was hungry, so I was going to get him a sandwich. This big guy was making fun of us, so I walked over to him. I was smoking a cigar and put it out on his forehead; Bobby got up and ran to get my mother. I don't know why he did that, but I guess he thought there was going to be trouble.

I told that big boy, "You're laughing at the wrong people. We're going to hurt you," but I swear that guy was nothing but a sissy.

He didn't even get out of his chair. He had the biggest burn mark on his forehead that I had ever seen.

The kids used to get along pretty well. They would sit up on that hill, and we had a big pond up there. Bobby would play Jason, and he would scare the kids every time we left. He would go up there on that hill with a machete and scare them to death wearing a Jason mask to look like Jason. My dad really liked those kids, Bobby and Leigh. He treated them like his own grandchildren. In fact, he carried their pictures in his wallet till the day he died.

Then I remember Bobby didn't come home from school one day, and I had to find Bobby. Well, I called up to the schoolhouse, and I asked if Bobby had been in school that day. The principal answered the phone, and he didn't like me when I was in school. He told me he was there, and I asked him why he had to stay after school. He told me he didn't bring his books to school or to class, and that was why he had to stay after school.

"Well," I said, "he's a straight-A student. Evidently, he doesn't need a book."

So one word led to another, and he asked me, "If you were working for a carpenter and didn't bring your saw with you to work, should you still get a check come Friday?" He was trying to be a smartass.

So I told him, "This puts a whole knew outlook on this. I didn't know Bobby was getting a check. I'll be right up there, you son of a bitch."

A girl I used to go to school with was working in the office, and I said I wanted to know where my stepson was.

She said, "Leroy, the principal ran."

I said, "Which way did he go?"

So she told me, and I chased him. By that time, they had called the police on me. If I had caught him, shit was going to happen. But after that, I don't think Bobby stayed after school anymore.

Another of my boys, David, was in the Buckskin School in South Salem, and the bus driver's son got his leg pissed on. So he snatched my boy up and was going to give him a whipping. Well, my boy came home and told me. I went into the school, and I told that bus driver and the principal that I would break his fucking neck if he ever touched my boy, and they found out it wasn't even my boy. I don't know what they did to that bus driver, but he would never drive down our lane. I told him I was going to hurt him. The principal tried to shut the door, and I backed up my truck so he couldn't get away from me. That wasn't good either.

I should have handled it a little differently, but I didn't care.

At this time, I was still drinking; I went to Hillsboro with my friend Ralph Brust to drink some beer. I told Darlene I'd be back in a little bit. I didn't do that too often without Darlene. Well I got over there; this big old boy wouldn't leave me alone, and Ralph was a chickenshit. Ralph's brother Tom and his wife Vicky were there. This boy told me he was in the army, and he ate snails, nails, and all kinds of junk. So we went back there, played pool, and had a shot of whisky. When that big son of a bitch came through that doorway, I hit him with a 22 pool stick and split his head wide open. I swear to God it looked like you could see his brain thumping, but it probably wasn't. So Vicky came and tackled me, Tom tackled Vicky, and I ran. They flew that guy out of there to Columbus, and I thought for sure that I killed that man. I'm glad I didn't. When he got out of the hospital a couple months later, he ran into Tom—that's Ralph's brother—and he told Tom to tell me there were no hard feelings. He thought he was Mr. Big Shit, and a little man put him in his place. He said he deserved everything I did to him, and that was a new one on me.

I was drinking again. I went to Jim and Alma's, and Darlene stayed home. I sat down with my cousin Dusty, and there was a girl sitting there.

She said, "I don't like you, and I never did." Then she told me she was going to slap me.

I told her, "If you slap me, I'm going to hit you back."

Well, she slapped me, and I knocked her out. I went to jail for that. The bartender and I got into a pretty good fight, and he called the police. I think I did three days in jail. I went and got Darlene, and they wanted fifty dollars to let me in and fifty dollars to let me back out.

So I said, "Well, I can solve that problem. I don't want to go in."

That was they only time I went to jail since I had been with Darlene. This time I was really planning on stopping, doing what I was doing. And believe it or not, when I got with Darlene, I slowed down ninety percent with what I used to do. At this time, I really settled down a lot.

One time, on the way home from Greenfield—we were living at the old farmhouse next to Maynard Ward—this black dog was following behind the car. We picked him up; he was just a pup, and we named him Spook. He was a black German Shepherd. Pete and Squirt would come down; Darlene and Squirt were walking down the road with the dog, and the dog brought them a groundhog. He would watch them in the woods, run to get them, and shake them, but he wouldn't kill them till you said it was all right. That was about the best dog we ever had, except he had the taste for blood, and he wanted to kill the chickens. We had a lot of chickens, and I got the idea to tie a chicken around his neck. I thought this would teach him not to kill them if it smelled real badly, but it didn't. He ate the chicken right off his neck.

Whitey Ward was our renter, and a week before he got sick, he was going to cut me off five acres to have a place to raise my kids. But he got sick and died. We had to move, so we moved to Turkey Ridge. That was when we bought our first trailer, and Uncle Pete helped us buy it. We paid him back every penny. He was good about lending us money when we needed it.

He always said, "I will lend it to you as long as you pay me back, but if you don't, the loans stop."

But we never failed to pay back any money. You can ask Squirt to this day, and she will tell you the same thing.

One night, Darlene, Mom, and I went to the bar, and while we were sitting there, some people from Knockemstiff, which is a very small town near

Greenfield, came in looking for trouble. I told them I didn't want any trouble; we were just having a beer. So they kept running their mouths at us, wanting to fight.

When he called my mother a bitch, I told him, "You got it."

So I called Daniel, my brother. These guys were very large men, 6'2" or 6'3".

When Daniel walked in, he asked me if that was all the help I called. I told him that's all I needed. At this time, I wanted to kill him for disrespecting my family. My friend Jimmy tried to stop me—he was the bartender—but we headed for the back door toward the alley. When we got to the back door, I was going to cut the one guy's throat, but someone bumped my arm and knocked the knife out of my hand. I didn't know where it went. So we started fighting, and we beat those men almost to death. I had skin hanging on my shoes; I kicked him so much and so hard.

He crawled to my mother and begged her, "Please. Don't let him hurt me no more. I'm sorry for calling you a bitch."

Daniel was still fighting the other man. So I went to help him, and he got mad. After it was all over, my brother Daniel said, "I'll never fight with you again; you don't fight fair."

I told him there was no fair way of fighting when you're my size.

The police officer said, "Roy, I think you've killed this one." But later on he told me he was glad we beat them up cause they kept coming to town causing trouble. "When I got the call it was you and Daniel, I knew it was you."

We were still living on Turkey Ridge in our trailer. Maynard's old girlfriend Frances was older, and she lived up on the hill from us. We were drinking some beer one day, and we went over there with them. These two guys came in, and they were beginning to get a little bit rowdy.

I took it for a little bit, and then I told Rome, "I took about all the shit I'm going to."

I went in, and the shit was on.

The next day I asked myself why we keep doing this; there had to be something better. And the only thing that got me to thinking that way was Darlene; I didn't like living that way anymore, and I wanted a change. I tried to get her to move, and she was afraid we couldn't make it. And we didn't have the money. So I saved up $1,500 to $2,000. I told her I thought we needed to move. She didn't like the idea, but she went to work that day and I called a truck. They hooked on that trailer and moved it to Washington Courthouse. I know it wasn't a big move, but it was a beginning.

We lived in that trailer court for a couple years, and I believe it was on Easter when Darlene was working and I was out drinking beer. I don't know what happened, but something went wrong with the water heater, and the trailer caught on fire. It burned that son of a bitch clear to the ground. We thought, *What in the name of God are we going to do?* But we had insurance.

They put us up in a motel—thank God—paid all of our bills, and bought a new trailer. By this time I couldn't read nor write, and I told Darlene I needed to learn to read and write. So I got in a class to read and write, and they taught me pretty well. I can't read really good, but good enough to get by. When I met Darlene, I couldn't read anything. I probably read at a first-grade level, and I'm probably at an eighth-grade level now.

Anyway, we stayed around Washington Courthouse for a while, and then I found some property in Chillicothe. We moved that trailer down there, and I think that was the beginning of our buying and selling property. Bobby had moved out and was living in Columbus. Leigh Ann was finishing up her senior year and wanted to stay in Greenfield to graduate with her friends. Every time one of the kids moved, it upset us, yet we wanted them to be able to make it on their own. I love those kids like my own.

Maynard set five to six hundred dollars on fire; he burnt it well. I picked up all that money and went out of there, and I kept it. I took it to the bank, and they gave good money for it. Because half of it was burnt, I said, "Maynard, why did you burn that money?"

He said, "So I can quit drinking."

One winter, we were stuck out there in the holler, and a blizzard came. It snowed and it snowed everybody in. So I walked over the mountain to go to the store cause you couldn't get the cars out. It was about a ten-mile hike, and I went over that hill. On the way back, I was about frozen to death, and the sheriff picked me up and took me as far as he could, which was pretty close to my house, just a couple of miles. I walked the rest of the way. I'll never do that again; I just about froze to death.

Another time Darlene and I went out for the evening, and we went down to the creek. The next time I saw her, she had poison ivy from head to foot. I didn't know she was allergic to it, and she looked like a lobster. I felt bad about that, and we didn't go back to the creek anymore. Actually it was at the Circle. That's what it was called.

A friends of ours—well, she was really Darlene's friend more than mine, but I knew her my whole life—told me that she would be the first to apologize. She didn't think Darlene and I would make it at long as we did. But I did turn my life around; Darlene is the only reason I turned my life around. I would probably be dead or in prison, one or the other.

I remember one day when all those kids had a turtle, and they were fighting over that damn turtle. I was sitting on the couch watching TV, and we had a wood stove. I took that turtle up and threw it in that stove. All those kids just looked at one another, and I said, "That's what you get for fighting over the turtle."

The kids never really gave us any problems, which was not what you would think. We couldn't eat at the table cause we didn't have enough chairs. So Roy built a picnic table with benches like the Waltons; we stained it and put polyurethane on it for a finish. It looked really nice, and everybody had a place to sit. We used that table for years, and it just fit that house. It was my dad's idea, and it worked.

Another time Rome Poole and I got into it out there on Haney Lane. I think it was around Christmas; we had a ham in the freezer in the back room. We left and came back, and Rome had stolen my ham and my turkey. He stole the whole dinner. Well, I went to Greenfield and I told Mom he stole my dinner.

She said, "No, he didn't."

I said, "Mom, if I look in that trash can and that ticket has been marked down with a black marker, that's my ham cause the man at the store did that for me."

She looked in the trash can, and there it was. They had the nerve enough to ask us to stay for dinner after stealing our food. That really made me mad. A week or two later, Rome came out to the house, trying to make up. I took a shotgun, and I blew the whole front of his truck off. I was trying to shoot him. He was the only person I believe I ever tried to kill. I just got mad because my kids didn't have a dinner. Well, we still had a dinner, but not what it would or could have been. Nor was it what we wanted. We had bought and paid for that.

Leigh Ann asked me one time why I spanked my kids, but never her when she did something wrong. She thought I didn't love her because I didn't spank her. I don't think those kids understood the way I was treated by my stepdad. I didn't want to be mean to them hurt them the way I had been hurt. Today, the way I was treated is still on my mind, and I don't think it will ever go away.

Leigh Ann was the most stubborn kid I have ever seen, I think. She just didn't take no for an answer. I would ground them, send them to their room, and do things like that. Finally, one day she did something—I don't remember what it was; it must have been pretty bad—and she finally got a butt whipping. I kept asking her to apologize, and she never would apologize. She finally did two or three days later.

Another time I stuck them all in a corner. They all had been bad, so I put all five of them in a corner. Then I gave them their chores to do. A little later, Bobby and little David came in the house. I had told them to clean the yard, and they came in and told me they were on strike—they must have gotten this from TV.

I sat there for a little bit, and I said, "No problem. All of you get in the corner until you come off strike. So they were all standing in that corner, and every one of them was mad at Bobby for talking about them going on strike. Leigh kept telling me she had to go to the bathroom, and I didn't believe her cause I wasn't going to keep her in the corner that long. She pissed on herself. The other kids thought that was so funny, but they never went on strike anymore.

Then one day I just asked Darlene if we ought to just get married; I wanted to make sure she wanted to be with me. We had been together about a year. I asked her because I didn't want her to have any doubts about whether she wanted to be with me. So we got married by Reverend Blaine in his house. We were living out in the country; we had chicken, pigs, and dogs. The pigs were going to be butchered and eaten. The pigs got big and the kids wouldn't eat them cause they became pets. They cried cause they thought I was going to butcher them. So I had to go sell them. They called the one Indian and the other American. Anyway, I talked Dad into putting them in back of his old van, and he took them to the market for us. I gave him some gas money. Kenny was staying with us at that time. He said okay, so he loaded them up. Those pigs shat all over that van, and he was so mad.

I guess, when I think about it, being with Darlene took me away from thinking about my childhood so much. For the first time in my life, I was really happy. Neither she nor I gave a damn about what anyone else thought. Nobody else paid our bills but her and me, and that's what I told her. Whatever they said we ignored it.

It really turned back to my childhood. I try to forget it, but I guess it's something that will stay there for the rest of my life. I don't know. I hope not.

There was a bunch of us who went out one night drinking wine. Earl May and I got drunk and pissed in a wine bottle, and I made him drink it. Then we got into a fight; Kenny thought that was really funny. The reason I did that was that he was downgrading people. He was married to Squirt, and Pete wasn't around so I took care of it.

Well, after the fire, we got us a new trailer, and it was in Washington Courthouse. I found a piece of property in Chillicothe, and they sold it on a land contract. So we moved our trailer; we were there for a good long while. Heather, our granddaughter, used to stay with us a lot. Dena and Larry were remodeling their house one time, and she stayed with us. I think it was two weeks or so. She really enjoyed that.

At this time, Darlene was working as a nurse's aide in Chillicothe, and I sat down one day and told her, "If you like this kind of work, just go to school and become a nurse."

Because Darlene had been talking to several nurses at work, she thought it would be a good move. But she didn't think we could afford it. I was on disability at that time and wasn't supposing to work. I think Darlene was only making $4.00 or $5.50 an hour maybe. When she started out as a nurse's aide, we had her children and my children. It wasn't easy. But we always saw that nobody went hungry and the children all dressed like everyone else.

Darlene was able to get into Hocking College with student loans and working part-time, as well as taking care of the kids and house. Everyone helped. It took two years, but she graduated and became an LPN. She could have gone three more quarters to become an RN. But the family needed to have the financial help at that time.

Then Utalcia, my oldest, was giving us fits. She would go down to the store, which was a little market, and get candy. We sent her after milk one day, and she came back with a baby. She had met a boy down around the store area, and she came back pregnant. I didn't know how, from my house to the little store, that she got that way, but she did. She was afraid to tell me. Darlene got up to go to school one morning, and she had her sweater on the table in the kitchen. When she picked up the sweater, this pregnancy test fell to the floor. Darlene came upstairs to tell me. Poor Talcia paid the price for that mistake. First of all, she had a miscarriage; it was hard on her cause it wouldn't abort on its own. She had to have a surgical procedure.

She was very upset that she had lost that baby. She still wanted to get married, but we weren't sure that was the thing to do. But she cried and carried on, so we let them get married. She was married in the church, and it was really nice. Then we let them move in the little shed out back. I fixed it up real nicely, and they fought all the time. I hated him because he played mind games with her. He was older than her. He was mean to her, and so was his family. In a way they thought they had to play Mom and Dad to her. But they didn't have to because she had me and Darlene, so they tried to correct her like a little child. That's when they moved in with the grandmother. There was a fight one night, and she called us. We went to the grandmother's—it wasn't far from where we lived—and she had had been cussing her and hit her. Roy would have liked to kill him, and he got so scared he pissed his pants. The sheriff came and the grandmother was upset, so we brought Talcia home with us. But she was gone by morning. He came during the night, and she went home with him. That shows you don't know a person like you think you do. I told the sheriff every time he whips my daughter, I'm going to whip him.

My other brother David hated him with a passion, and he was someone you didn't want to hate you because bad things could happen to you. I had to keep trying to keep him from hurting him.

One other time, we were sitting in the house, and they were arguing. David walked in the house, and I walked over and slapped her husband right in the mouth. I thought my brother was going to hurt him. And Talcia stayed with him for seven years. It put Darlene and I through seven years of hell, getting up at two in the morning, running to see if she was all right, and bringing her home. We lived in Columbus then, and she was always gone before I got out of bed.

When we were struggling to get Darlene through school, I knew she could do it. Finally, they put me on SSI, and that helped us get through. We got a check one day for five thousand dollars, and we thought we were rich. At least I thought I was. My Uncle Pete was dealing in drugs then; I believe he got caught doing it. My cousin Rowdy was running around this policeman, but he didn't know he was a policeman, even though I kept telling him. The guy came to my house, and he and Rowdy were sitting there talking. He asked me all kinds of questions, like where did I get my house and my nice furniture?

I would look him right in the eye and tell him right to his face, "You're a cop."

He would say, "No, I'm not."

I said, "Yes, you are."

I would tell everybody he was a cop. We walked into my friend Jack Daugherty's house cause Jack was going to buy a dog from him. We stood there and I told Jack right in front of him that he was a cop, a narc. Jack just looked at me. He was always asking too many questions.

It wasn't too long after that he arrested Jack. He was a cop. Rowdy and I were with him one night. We were drinking with him, and we were going down this country road. He kept trying to smoke marijuana, which I never did smoke—I never did like it. I've never done drugs' I've always been a drunk.

He was going pretty fast, around ninety or one hundred miles an hour, and I pulled this knife. I reached up around his throat and told him, "If we wreck, I'm going to cut your head clear off."

My cousin Rowdy looked at me, raised his hands up in the air, and said, "My mommy told me not to run around with you, Roy. Because you're crazy."

I was going to kill that cop that night, and Rowdy stopped me. He was trying to force drugs on me, and come to think about it, I had never seen a cop smoke pot continuously, even when somebody else wasn't smoking it.

We had tried to sell that trailer and had no luck. Then one day, out of the clear blue, our real-estate lady called. It was on New Year's Eve. They had a lady who wanted a one-time look at the trailer cause the contract had run out with the real-estate people. We said yes. Well low and behold, the lady bought it. We had wanted to buy the house on the corner when that lady moved because it was a nice big house. It needed some work, but it could be fixed up nicely. Anyway, the lady wanted possession of the trailer pretty quickly, and the man who owed all that property had a barn that had been renovated. He said we could stay there till we could get in the house.

Anyway, we moved in the house; we stayed there for two or three years and fixed it up. That was where we lived when Talcia got married, and Koeby was born when we lived there also.

We had an Akita dog, he was a really good guard dog. We lived right beside the highway—that was why we had him; it was the freeway. A truck driver broke down, and there were signs on the gate and fence that said to beware of the dog. So he climbed over the fence, and the dog almost ate him up before I could get to him.

I told him to let me call the police, but he said, "No, I'm all right," and he hobbled back to his truck. But he was bleeding pretty good. He got what he deserved, I guess. The signs were there.

Another time we were lying in bed, and it was late at night. We heard the most awful crash. We got up, and there was an RV and two other cars. Bodies were everywhere on the freeway, along with life flight, fire trucks, and emergency vehicles. Helicopters were looking in our yard for people who were ejected from their cars. We had to keep the kids inside so they couldn't see it.

We had a lot of good times; I had more good times with Darlene than bad. I didn't want to get in trouble anymore. But it is hard to shake bad habits.

I guess it was in that house when I started in carpentry work. Dad had taught me a little bit; I knew some. That's when I started overhauling houses, I guess. I started remodeling. I changed the entry cause when you walked into the house you could see right up the steps. I closed it off and put the steps around the corner. It looked really nice. I did that when Darlene was at work one day. Everybody liked it. It even made the living room look better. I had to use old wood out of the barn because we didn't have the money to buy new. That was probably one of the best houses we ever lived in. It was laid out really nicely with a large living room and a country kitchen. The stairs went upstairs from the kitchen, and another set was in the living room. There was a bath upstairs, and a bath downstairs that I put in. But I just wasn't smart enough then to know what to do with it.

By this time Bobby and Leigh had moved out. They were both married. I talked Darlene into moving to Columbus. My dad didn't want me to do so; he wanted me to stay there. I think he thought I couldn't make it. At the time, Darlene didn't want to try it either. So we sold the house, took the money, and moved to Columbus. I told her I wanted to get the kids out of there; I didn't want them raised there. It was no place to raise children. Every person I knew and their children had been in jail or in trouble. In that little hick town, there was nothing to do, nowhere to go.

I never lived in a city before, and it worried me a little bit when I got up there. I didn't know if I could make it or not.

I ended up working at a store up there, and I worked for about a year. And one day I said, *This isn't for me.* I need to find something better to do than this. I found another job; I started in construction.

After we first moved up there, I thought to myself, *I've made a mistake,* and then I thought, *let me give it a chance first.* I kept thinking about my kids getting in trouble down where we used to live in Greenfield.

So we moved in with Leigh Ann, and we stayed there for two or three months. Then we bought a condo in Hilliard, and that's when I found a job doing stonework. I saw these people doing this one day, and I thought, *I would like to try that.*

I saw an ad in the paper, went and put an application in, and got hired. He hired me as a laborer, and I told him I would like to learn to lay the stone. He said that took a very long time—a year or two—before you can really do it. In six months, I was hanging more stone than anyone he had working for him, and I became the foreman. That's when I was making pretty good money, and so was Darlene. That's when we first started taking vacations. The first one I ever had in my life was with Darlene. We grabbed up David and Stacy; Talcia, Leigh, and Bobby were already gone, so we took those two and went to Tennessee. David and Stacy didn't like it a bit; it wasn't good. We gave them money to buy what they wanted, we had a motel on our first stop that had a carnival, and they wouldn't go unless we did. We had given them several hundred dollars for each to spend while we were there. Then we got to Gatlinburg, and they just didn't like it or Cherokee, North Carolina. Stacy wanted to go do things, but she was scared without David. David didn't want to do anything. They did like going out to eat and things, and they enjoyed the rides at Dollywood. He wanted to be back home with his friends. They had their own motel room, a pool, and everything; we just couldn't make them happy. Davey sat on the edge or side of the bed the whole time we were there.

Then one day, he came home and David said, "Dad, these boys jumped me and beat me up."

So I found out the boy's dad's name, and I called him up. I told him that his son and two or three other boys beat my boy up. I blew up and I called him all kind of bad names. I told him to come over to the house so I could beat him up cause his boy was chickenshit for three or four people to jump on one. But the guy kept apologizing to me; it wasn't his fault. I just got mad and was going to take it out on someone. So I tried to take it out on him.

When we got up there, we had a little trouble with Darlene's ex-husband. He told Heather I wasn't her grandpa, and I was not related to her. That made Dena and Larry really mad. There was no call for that. All I've ever been is good to his children and his grandchildren. I was there when he wasn't, but it wasn't that we tried to keep him from them. He just didn't come around. But neither did my ex-wife. Heather asked me that day—she was just a little old thing—if I was her grandpa, and I said, "Well, who do you think I am?"

She said, "Pappy."

"Then that's who I am." And we never brought it up again.

When we moved up here, Darlene started making really good money because she finally graduated. I think that's another reason why we left Chillicothe; she couldn't make as much money as she could in Columbus. She ended up getting a really good job and making good money, and I was making decent money. We were living really good living, better than I ever had in my life without stealing. At this time, everything I was doing was legal.

When we were in the condo, we decided to build a house in Apple Valley by the lake. We lived there for a little over a year. Darlene's ex-husband filed bankruptcy and didn't tell Darlene, and it came back on her. So we had to file bankruptcy, so we let that house go back and kept the condo.

We moved back into the condo. At the time, I was still working for the stone company, Darlene was still doing nursing, and David and Stacy were still at home. This was the time Leigh Ann and Mike were getting a divorce, and Leigh Ann and Koeby moved in with us. David was getting his driver's license; we had a Tracker, and he practiced all the time when we lived in Mount Vernon. He drove that thing round and round where that house was about 10,000 times a day. I tried to teach him, but I didn't have the patience. So I sent him to driver's ed.

I remember one time when Koeby probably wasn't but five years. He went to school, and they where having share day. He asked his teacher if he could bring his pap. The teacher thought that was cute.

We were back in the condo. I was coming home one night from work, and the police were there. I thought, *Well, what has happened?* I went up there to see what the problem was, and there were two girls there fighting over David. I asked the officer what the problem was, and he explained it to me.

I asked David, "What are you going to do."

He said, "I don't care. I don't want either one of them." He walked in the house and up the steps to his room, and that was the end of it.

Then he was going with this one girl and broke up with her. Her parents came over and asked Darlene and me to have him go back with her. I told them that wasn't how life worked. We weren't going to pick who he went with. Then he hooked up with the wife he has now. I kind of didn't want him to because Stacy was going with her brother. So I just let it go and let them do whatever they wanted to do. He stayed with her for about five years. Then they finally got married.

Then Darlene kept asking my daughter Stacy, my youngest, if anything was happening between her and Scott. She said hat she would put her on birth-control pills. She said, "We don't even kiss."

So to this day, we don't know how Scotty got here—that's my grandson—because God only knows they didn't even kiss. So we went to Scott's parents. At the time, I was really mad about this. I even thought about making her get an abortion. She thought I was, but I wasn't. I told her future in-laws that there's no way she could be pregnant because they don't even kiss. These people just didn't know what to do. To this day in 2006, they have never bothered us for money or anything. They have done really well on their own. I thought she would be the one who I would have to help all the time.

We told Leigh Ann that she had to save up her money to get an apartment, and my son-in-law Larry told me she was sitting at the bar for drinks—and one of the bars in Plain City—about every Friday night. They had a little argument, but I took care of it. I went and rented her an apartment. First I asked her how much money she had saved up, and she didn't have any. It was about time for income taxes, so we rented the apartment and she paid us back when she got her taxes. It was the idea of trying to make the kids responsible. My ex-wife was still never paying for the children, and Darlene's ex wasn't either. We both had good jobs at this time, and we didn't really care. We were making it pretty good.

We helped David buy a car. We were sitting at home one night, and when he came, the whole exhaust from the manifold back had fallen off of it.. I know what happened; he hit something, a ditch or a hill, and tore it off. He tried to tell me it just fell off. Two weeks later, he came and had the clutch pedal in his hand. He had called Darlene, and she went to pick him up. He was carrying the pedal in his hand. So they left the car there till I got home. I said I had never seen one of them fall off in my life. He thought his old dad was silly, but his old dad forgot more than he knew.

At this time Bobby was getting along pretty well. After Talcia's divorce from Shad, she married her second husband Timmy. They don't have any children together, but he is really good to the children, thank God.

Every one of my grandchildren is very special to me. My stepgrandchildren are loved as well as my own grandchildren. I don't see any difference between them; I feel the same about all of them. Heather has always been very special to me, ever since she was born. The rest of the grandchildren get a little jealous about that. I try not to play any favorites. I probably do once in a while, but I don't mean to do so.

Well, when it was time for Davey to graduate from high school, he was going over to the now in-laws to eat. Davey was the only one of my kids to graduate, and I'm so proud of that boy for that. I think he is the only Bennett to graduate. Stacy had to quit school cause she got pregnant—God only knows how; she never even kissed boys. But it happened. I thought about calling *Ripley's Believe It or Not*. She never had sex, never kissed, and got a baby.

Talcia's first husband was really mean to his children; the only one he ever cared about was the first one, Andrea. He was mean to the boys, and his family was kind of mean to the boys too. They would let Andrea go down and play, and they would make the boys stay home, stand at the fence, and watch. Then I would get mad, and I kind of think it's the same way to this day. But that little Shad is about the best worker I've ever seen in a little kid. He works with you the whole day and never complains.

Boy, some of my life is really getting boring now. But I guess this is how regular people live.

We started camping down at Deer Creek and bought a camper. We met some friends, Jeff and Susan. I think it was around 1998; I'm not real sure. And we decided to build a house in and around Clarksburg, so we rented the condo out, moved all our belongings—except everyday clothes and such—put everything else in storage, and lived at the campgrounds. That sure was an experience. We stayed there from May till the end of September or first of October, when the weather started turning cold. While we were living at the campground, our trailer caught on fire. That was a really bad situation cause that was where we were living while I was building the house. Uncle Pete used to come to the campground to visit; he really loved it there. He would go in the camper and go to sleep. He was getting pretty sick at that time. He could hardly do anything or go anywhere. He had arthritis and heart problems. He was in bad shape.

I was down at my sister Georgie's, and my mother was cleaning out her refrigerator and had a heart attack. She ended up getting open-heart surgery. That was when she really started going down hill; she just kept having surgeries of all kinds for different things. She has many things wrong with her. It worries me every day that something is going to happen to her.

My brother Daniel kept thinking my father Kenny Bennett wasn't his dad. I didn't know any differently whether he was or he wasn't, but Mom finally told him. He was forty-two years old when she told him who his dad was. It about killed Daniel, and it still bothers him to this day that they had that secret all this time.

We all used to go to the Eagle's; Jake and Joyce, Gary Smith, Daniel, Dad, Darlene, and I. We used to really have a good time. We would go see them on Sundays and eat dinner. We really enjoyed that. One time, we were at Jake's having a picnic, and my daughter Talcia and some of the other kids went up to the corner store and stole some sprinkles like you would put on a cake. I don't know why she would want to steal them. She had money and quite a bit for all the kids to get something. Stacy came running back to Joyce and Jake's, and she was crying. She couldn't even talk to get out of her what was wrong. She finally told me, so I went up to the store. The store owner knew, and he told me he would have to call the police.

I was about half drunk so I whispered to him, "You do what you have to do, son of a bitch, and later on, I'll do what I have to do."

But I didn't want my daughter hear me say that. She might think it was okay to steal.

But if they would have filed charges on my daughter, she was only ten at the most. The boogieman was going to get him. But he finally let her go, and she got in trouble when she got home. When the policeman was there, her legs where shaking so badly; her knees were knocking together. She said some little girl at school told her she stole all the time; that's why she did that.

To this day, I don't know if she has stolen since. That scared her badly. I'm glad my kids didn't follow in my footsteps. I pray to God all the time. It wouldn't be good.

I remember I was doing some stonework when I got a call on my cell phone that my Aunt Edna had died. It felt like everything in my body just drained away. I thought the world of that woman. But we knew she was sick, and it was going to happen. Before she went, she got right with God.

It wasn't long after that when I had trouble with my heart. I had to have a heart cath. Darlene always thought it was because of that house I built cause I worked in that house for fifteen hours a day for a year. Most of the work was done by me. Davey helped when he could, but he had a job too. Bobby also helped me a little bit. We ended up selling that house and moved back to the condo in Hilliard. Then, after we moved back, I worked for the carpenter's union. For a while, that guy I met at the campgrounds and I were building bridges up around Springfield. So I did that for a while; then I started building houses on my own. And I had a man who worked for me who was an alcoholic, and he just about got me sued. But nothing bad happened, and I thank God for that. I got rid of him. It was me, him, and my boy David climbing up on those houses, and he was drunk all the time. Or he wouldn't show up, so we just gave it up. But I'm still working on my own. I remodel houses. I do anything to a house that needs doing. I can usually figure it out or find someone who knows how to do it.

Then, not a couple years after Aunt Edna died, we got the call that Uncle Pete had died. That about killed my mother. Then, not long after that, my mother's other sister Mamie died. And now my mother is the only one left out of that side of the family.

I was always close to all my family; we were raised around each other. It took me a long time to get over it when Pete died because he wasn't just an uncle; he was a close friend. We did a lot together.

Then I remember one time we were at an Eagle's picnic. Uncle Jake and I were drinking some beer. He sat on the edge of this guy's tailgate and passed out. This guy was from Springfield—that we knew—and I looked and there went Jake in the back of the truck asleep. I hollered, and my Aunt Joyce hollered, "There goes Jake."

So I got in the car and flagged down the other car.

He said, "What's wrong?"

I said, "You have Uncle Jake in the back."

I just kept thinking if he woke up and stepped out the back, he would die. And that probably what would have happened. Anyway I got him.

Darlene and I spent a lot of time at Jake and Joyce Smith's house. We spent years there. They weren't just relations; they were friends, and great people, and a lot of fun. They would give you the shirts off their backs. And they still will.

By this time, I was really slowing down about getting into trouble. Thank God. I was just happy with my marriage; we got along really well and still do.

Even though we lived in Columbus, we still would go to Greenfield about every weekend to visit my family: my mom, Joyce, and Jake. Then, when we got to doing our vacations, I was really glad of that. We really needed them. I had never had a vacation with nobody in my life. At least, I never had what you could call a vacation. I've been to California and Florida, but I was usually running from the law.

It took me a long time to get used to holding a steady job, just coming home and eating supper, and watching TV. It wasn't a bad thing; it just was a whole different life for me.

To this day, people tell me if it wasn't for Darlene, I would probably be dead or in prison, and I believe it. I believe it with all my heart.

I still sit and think about the old days. I don't reckon they will ever leave me. I don't think about it as much as I used to. I guess I'll never get over my childhood.

I think about when we were still in Chillicothe. I was sent to Ohio State University because I blacked out a lot. I never understood why. So I was in there about seven to ten days. We found out I had a cyst on my brain and was having seizures. The way it was explained; the cyst was in the center of the brain and was inoperable. I had an illness when I was an infant called meningitis, and my dad had remembered. I guess I was in Children's Hospital for a long time. My dad said my doctor at the time was Doctor Seymour. I told my doctor at Ohio State, and they were able to retrieve my records from that far back. But that was the cause of the seizures. It probably was the reason for some of my behavior while growing up, if the truth is known. I take medication now and have for quite a few years. I also have a sleep disorder. Anyway where the cyst is they said it would kill me if they tried to remove it.

Anyway, when I was in the hospital getting all those tests done, this guy kept telling me he was gay, and I told him not to come back in my room or touch me for any reason. I didn't want that dreaded disease those people got. So the doctor called my wife Darlene and asked her if she would please come up and talk to me cause I wouldn't let one of the male nurses take care of me. Everything would have been fine if he hadn't told me he was gay.

But I was glad that they found out what was wrong with me anyway. I've been blacking out my whole life, but they said it was from the meningitis I had as an infant. I just thought everyone did that. The doctor told me it could still be fatal if it starts growing.

When I left the hospital, they gave me pills I need to take every day. They didn't help much, but I still take them. I don't notice any changes. They say it has to be in my blood system. I take them.

My sister Georgie got hurt at work, and she's turned into a drug addict. She takes all kinds of medications whether she needs them or not. I think she's in better shape than she lets on to be. All she wants is the oxycontin. And God only knows, she sure takes a lot of them. She slobbers at the mouth, and I can't understand her half the time.

Darlene's sister is always really nice to me. We all get along really well, especially with Hubie. I used to really like Hubie before he passed away. He was a good old boy. I think we clicked together because we were both hillbilly boys.

From the condo, we just started buying and selling our homes. We were fixing them up and reselling them, and we made some pretty good money on them. Darlene hates moving though. She gets mad at me every time. I fix up this one house on Warfield Drive in Grove City, and I did such a makeover on it that they put it in *The Columbus Dispatch* newspaper as the most improved house in the block. It was a pretty nice neighborhood. We made pretty good money off that house when we sold it.

From there I think, we went to 62 and Harrisburg Pike in Harrisburg. I added a big garage to that house and remodeled the whole house. It wasn't supposed to be in a flood zone, but it was. That was the biggest nightmare of a house that I've ever had in my life. We looked out the window one morning, the water was rolling so fast, and a small building came through the yard. And it hit the tree. So we threw a fit. We sued the people who sold us the house for not telling or disclosing that it was in a flood zone. We ended up getting paid. We then sold the house for a lot more than what we had in it. I told the people who purchased the house that it was in a flood zone, and they didn't seem to care. So much for that. I just wanted to be rid of it. Then we bought a small condo in Piper Meadows on the west side.

Back to the family, it wasn't too much longer after Mamie died that my Uncle Jake passed away. That really bothered me. He was a very, very close friend of mine. I didn't think I was going to be able to handle that one very well. But I did.

The boys woke up one morning, and they came downstairs and went into the kitchen. They were talking to him; he was at the table with his cup of coffee like he always was every morning. He had the stove on; he always lit the stove to take the chill off of the kitchen. He was always cold. Anyway, Jake didn't answer the boys; they went over and touched him, and he was dead. He was ice cold, just sitting there. Old Jake was my supervisor out at the graveyard.

One time, we were all working at the graveyard burying people, and we got so drunk we couldn't bury this man. The vault man was so drunk that he couldn't put the vault on. He passed out on the vault; then came Dad and my cousin Dick.

My dad threw a fit and said, "Who's going to bury this man? Look! You guys are drunk."

I thought that was the funniest thing I had ever seen in my life. Dad was just running around like a chicken with its head cut off, just preaching to us. We were just laughing at him. He was as serious as a heart attack. Finally Rick buried him; he worked there too. Jake was an employee there; I was in jail serving time and working for the city. I always got to go home every night.

I'm so glad those times of getting into trouble are over. That really tore my dad up when Jake died. Uncle Jim died first; then Jake died.

Uncle Jim died of cancer. He and Dad were close, but not like he was with Jake. It almost killed my dad.

Dad kept saying, "What am I going to do?"

He kept wanting to buy graves in a place out in the country, and they didn't mow it or anything. My brother David and I finally bought him a lot beside his brother Jake. That shut him up; at least he knew where he was going to be buried. He was happy cause it was going to be beside Jake.

I've had a lot of family pass on in these last few years. But I will get into that later. The doctors tell me that my heart isn't that good, and that bothers me sometimes. I'm not afraid of dying; I just don't want to leave Darlene or my grandchildren. So I'm going to call it a day on this tape.

Back to the children, Talcia had her first child with Shad; that was Andrea. I think she was sixteen. Then came Shad, and Jake was the last one. She stayed for a while, till Jake was about two or three years old, and then she finally divorced Shad, which was a blessing cause he treated her very badly. She then met Timmy and has been married for three to four years. They seem to be getting along very well. The children really like Timmy, especially Jake. He really loves Timmy. Talcia and Timmy both work and are living outside of Circleville. Talcia wants to go to nursing school; I hope she does.

Stacy is working to get her GED to better herself in a job, and she is still married to Scott. She has Scotty and Alisha. They're both in school now, and that makes it a little easier for her to get a better job. The have a trailer they bought and are getting rid of; they recently moved in with Scott's mom.

David is still married to Christy, and they have Andrew. He is in school also now. They just moved in with Christy's mom, who is Scott's sister. David is working in maintenance, and Christy works at a vet's office.

Leigh and Lenny both work at OfficeMax. They have Koeby and Nicholas. Kobey visits his dad sometimes. Lenny is his stepdad, and he is very good to Koeby. Nicholas is Leigh Ann's second child; his father is Lenny. They all seem to get along very well.

Bobby is married to Christa, and they have two children, Lorna and David. They live here in Columbus. Both children are in school. Lorna is into cheerleading, and David plays football and baseball. They are a very active family.

Dena, the oldest, has made a very good job and lifestyle for herself; she has two stepchildren—twins—and two children of her own. Her husband has his own construction company. Dena travels all over the world. She owns two homes. Two of the children are out of school, Melissa and Melinda. Heather is in college, and Jessica is still at home in high school.

So when this family gets together, it is quite a clan.

Well, we're about the end of this book. The kids are all grown and gone, and they have their own children. Darlene and I are all by ourselves. We take a lot of vacations, which was something I never got to do in my life. Darlene's daughter Dena gets us a really expensive rooms when we go out of state or out of the country. We really appreciate her for doing that. We could never afford that. We couldn't have vacations as long as we do. Instead of taking short ones, we take long one! It's always at a five-star hotel.

Heather, my girl, is in college now to become a nurse practitioner, and I'm so proud of her for that. We see all fourteen grandkids all the time for the most part. We used to have cookouts with all the children and grand-children, as well as holiday dinners.

Since David and Stacy married brother and sister, they just don't come around for holidays or cookouts like I wish they would. That hurts my feelings, but there's not a whole lot you can do. Other than that, life is great with all the kids.

Leigh Ann never did give a shit. She always called the shots. Sometimes I wonder how a man ever lives with her; she is so mean. Darlene says she is the most like me out of all the kids, and she isn't even my blood. She calls us every day and checks on her mother and me.

During last vacation we went on, we went to my brother David's. He moved to Tennessee near Gatlinburg. We took my mom and Koeby, and they had such a good time. They just laughed all the way down and back. We had Koeby up on this mountain, and he had to pee. Finally I let him out of the back of the car so he could go to the bathroom. He had to pee so bad his legs were shaking. He turned around and there was a whole motorcycle gang watching Kobe pee. He said his legs where shaking like Elvis. Mom and David thought that was so funny. They laughed till they cried.

We have been buying and selling houses for the last fourteen years, but we are about to come to an end. My health isn't that good. I'm going to have to stop, but the money was good; the ride was good while it lasted.

We ended up with a lot of nice homes, and we spent a lot of good money. So, kids, it's all gone. Ha. But we have gone all over the country, and on cruises; we had a good time. I'll soon be fifty years old in July, and Darlene will be sixty-five in August. I think it's time we quit working so much and just kind of kick back and travel some more. This is about the end of the book. I hope all you kids enjoy it cause I wrote it for all the grand-children. So they can remember me when I'm gone and Darlene is too.

This is the end of my life story as I remember it.
George Leroy Bennett